ISSUE 16, OCTOBER 2022

AUSTRALIAN FOREIGN AFFAIRS

Contributors

Melissa Conley Tyler is executive director of the Asia-Pacific Development, Diplomacy & Defence Dialogue (AP4D).

Geraldine Doogue presents *Saturday Extra* and *Extra* on ABC RN, with an editorial focus on foreign affairs.

Gwynne Dyer is an independent journalist whose twice-weekly column on international affairs appears in more than twenty countries.

Cherie Lagakali is senior advisor at the GFCE Pacific Hub.

Greg Lockhart is a Vietnam veteran and an Australian historian and writer. His memoir *Weaving of Worlds: A Day on Île d'Yeu* is forthcoming.

Geoff Raby is a former ambassador to China and a regular contributor to *The Australian Financial Review*.

Laura Tingle is chief political correspondent of the ABC's *7.30* program and a former political editor of *The Australian Financial Review*.

Erin Watson is founder and managing director of Baker & York, specialising in international public affairs and public policy.

Jeffrey Wilson is director of research and economics at the Australian Industry Group.

Australian Foreign Affairs is published three times a year by Schwartz Books Pty Ltd. Publisher: Morry Schwartz. ISBN 978-1-76064-3478 ISSN 2208-5912 Subscriptions – 1 year print & digital auto-renew (3 issues): $49.99 within Australia incl. GST. 1 year print and digital subscription (3 issues): $59.99 within Australia incl. GST. 2 year print & digital (6 issues): $114.99 within Australia incl. GST. 1 year digital only auto-renew: $29.99. Payment may be made by MasterCard, Visa or Amex, or by cheque made out to Schwartz Books Pty Ltd. Payment includes postage and handling. To subscribe, fill out the form inside this issue, subscribe online at www.australianforeignaffairs.com, email subscribe@australianforeignaffairs.com or phone 1800 077 514 / 61 3 9486 0288. Correspondence should be addressed to: The Editor, Australian Foreign Affairs, 22–24 Northumberland Street, Collingwood, VIC, 3066 Australia Phone: 61 3 9486 0288 / Fax: 61 3 9486 0244 Email: enquiries@australianforeignaffairs.com. Editor: Jonathan Pearlman. Deputy Editor: Kate Morgan. Associate Editor: Chris Feik. Consulting Editor: Allan Gyngell. Digital Editor and Marketing: Alexandra Turnbull. Editorial intern: Emma Hoy. Management: Elisabeth Young. Subscriptions: Sam Perazzo. Publicity: Anna Lensky. Design: Peter Long. Production Coordination: Marilyn de Castro. Typesetting: Tristan Main. Cover photograph: Patrick Semansky / Associated Press. Printed in Australia by McPherson's Printing Group.

Editor's Note

THE RETURN OF THE WEST

Australia's most recent foreign policy white paper was released in 2017 – five years before Vladimir Putin invaded Ukraine – but was impressively prescient about the prospect of a Russian-initiated war in Europe.

At a time when much of the world was questioning the relevance of NATO, the white paper warned that Russia's "destabilising" conduct had made NATO more important to security in Europe than at any time since the end of the Cold War. "Russia's policies affect Australia both directly and indirectly," it said. "Australia will work with partners to resist Russia's conduct when it is inimical to global security."

This blunt assessment stemmed from Australia's tragic experience of Putin's adventurism. The white paper was written as Canberra was pressing Moscow to cooperate with investigations into the downing of Malaysia Airlines flight MH17, which was hit by a Russian-made missile over Ukraine, killing all 298 passengers, including thirty-eight Australians. The missile was fired by Russian-backed separatists and allegedly belonged to Russia's 53rd Anti-Aircraft Missile Brigade.

As Australia's diplomats and intelligence agencies predicted, Putin's destabilising conduct has continued, with far-reaching consequences. The invasion of Ukraine in February has disrupted food and energy supplies, led to NATO's expansion, prompted a forty-plus-country effort to provide arms and aid to Ukraine, and resulted in the imposition of the world's most extensive economic sanctions.

But the white paper failed to predict (how could it?) how profoundly Putin's actions in Ukraine would disrupt the global order, and shake the tenets on which Australia's foreign policy outlook is based.

In recent years, Australia has championed the international rules-based order, which has been seen as a safeguard against developments such as China's assertiveness and rising protectionism. But the war in Ukraine is now testing one of the white paper's basic assumptions – that this rules-based order, which has done so much to ensure Australia's prosperity and security since World War II, can yet be preserved.

The invasion is raising questions about the reliability of the global free trade system; it is highlighting the obstacles that countries such as the United States, Australia and Japan face as they try to build partnerships to counter China's ambitions; and it is showing, yet again, that the outcomes of wars are difficult to predict, even when initiated by great military powers. The invasion has put on display the differences in outlook between Australia and rising Asian powers such as India, which did not support the United Nations' condemnation of the invasion and has gladly bought the Russian fuel rejected by the West, and Indonesia, which supported the UN resolution but has avoided directly criticising or punishing Russia.

The invasion has emboldened Europe and led to a renewed solidarity between Washington and Brussels, but it has also demonstrated that this united front has limited support beyond traditional allies such as Australia. And so "the West" – a construct which should have little place in a genuinely global rules-based order – has made a comeback.

Shortly after the invasion, then prime minister Scott Morrison claimed that liberal democracies were being pitted against a "new arc of autocracy". But the war is actually a reminder that neat binary divisions don't work, and that states are slippery and that their interests derive from a mix of calculations, of which morality is often just one.

The war in Ukraine is not only causing devastation in Europe but has triggered new and intensifying challenges to the global order. It is crucial for Australia to examine the consequences of this unfolding tragedy – to assess the ways in which it is undermining Canberra's foreign policy aspirations and is reshaping the prospects for stability, security and prosperity in Asia and beyond.

Jonathan Pearlman

UKRAINE FALLOUT

Australia and the new world disorder

Geoff Raby

It's hard to imagine how bizarre it would have seemed just one year ago for a new Australian prime minister to be making a speech in the Ukrainian capital, Kyiv, or visiting the nearby town of Bucha.

During the past forty years, a new Australian prime minister would have been expected to visit several major Asian capitals and Washington, if not London, to open their account. Malcolm Fraser was the first to begin his term with visits to Tokyo and Beijing, before visiting Washington and London. He was a leader of his time and understood how important Asia had become for Australia's future.

While Albanese visited Tokyo for a multilateral meeting and Jakarta for a long-programmed ministerial meeting, the first discretionary bilateral visit of his term was Paris, followed by Ukraine. And that was after he was the first Australian leader to attend a NATO summit meeting. This underscores how much, and how suddenly, the world order has changed, including for Australia, with the return of war to the European continent.

Yet Russia's invasion is both symptomatic of the changed order and a product of it. Russia did what it did because it could. Moreover, it has not flinched in the face of massive, coordinated Western sanctions. With the rise of China and authoritarian states being more assertive in the face of declining US influence, multipolarity has returned. And the war in Europe will leave China in a stronger position, even as it unifies the West. This is something Canberra has largely failed to recognise or, if it has, to respond to creatively.

China arrives

Putin's invasion of Ukraine has brought to a juddering halt the narrative that the last vestiges of the old rules-based order could still peacefully guide the relations between states, while underpinning economic integration between them.

The rules-based order has long been under challenge. Ironically, its greatest defender has often been its greatest threat. The United States has flouted the rules with impunity when its interests didn't align. The illegal and immoral invasion of Iraq in 2003 was just one of many episodes. The message to authoritarian regimes is that there are different standards for different states, and ultimately might is right.

The Trump administration took this to a reckless level, most notably with its attacks on the WTO. The effort to undermine the rules-based trading system by refusing to appoint new Appellate Body judges has continued under the Biden administration. The historical irony is that, of all the trade mechanisms laboriously negotiated during the seven years of the Uruguay Round of multilateral talks, none reflected US interests more than the WTO dispute settlement system. Designed and pushed by the United States, it introduced a form of black-letter law into the international trade system that had never been seen before. It was the chapeau of the rules-based order.

But it was not just America that weakened the order it had created and led. Long before Putin's invasion of Ukraine, the world's unipolar moment had ended. China's rise meant that another great power could challenge US primacy, not directly through military engagement, but through its economic weight, technology and diplomacy.

From the early 2010s, during Obama's second term, the US's stance towards China changed from cooperation to competition. Obama announced the "Pivot to Asia", but, beyond the rhetorical flourish, it lacked substance. Perhaps the first clear indicator of the US's change of approach occurred in 2014 when it openly opposed China's initiative to create the Asian Infrastructure Investment Bank (AIIB) and urged allies not to join.

The episode was the first time an Australian government had been confronted with an explicit choice between the United States and China, a choice which successive governments believed they would never be asked to make. Until then, Australia had supported China's efforts to reform the Bretton Woods institutions of the IMF and World Bank, despite resistance from the US and the Europeans. These institutions were increasingly looking anachronistic. They were unable to take account adequately of how the balance of economic power had changed irrevocably with the rise of China, of East Asia and the emerging market economies. Australia had led the push for reform, as the former treasurer Peter Costello stated in 2007, because it believed in "the need to recognise the growing economic weight of ... key countries in the Asian region".

America would have to choose how to respond to China's rise

Initially, Australia, led by Prime Minister Tony Abbott, also welcomed China's initiative to create the AIIB. Australia had been the first developed country China consulted on membership. The two countries were also well advanced in their negotiation of a bilateral FTA.

Obama and Secretary of State Hillary Clinton drew a line in the sand on China over the AIIB. Enormous pressure was applied to countries such as Australia, Japan and Canada not to join. The Australian Cabinet was split. Six months later, the Abbott government reluctantly joined. By then, most European states had joined, diminishing Australia's potential influence as an early mover. It would be the last occasion on which Australia supported a Chinese-led economic or diplomatic initiative.

Within China, the US's opposition to the AIIB reinforced the conviction that the United States would always oppose China's sharing in global leadership. In a rare act of contrition, the US's principal, or at least self-proclaimed, architect of the "Pivot", Kurt Campbell, now President Biden's Indo-Pacific affairs coordinator, conceded in his 2016 memoir that Washington's position on the AIIB had been a mistake.

Whether China's behaviour towards other states would have been different had the US embraced its initiatives – especially the Belt and Road Initiative (BRI) – more constructively is of course moot. China's increasingly assertive behaviour in the South China Sea predates the elevation of Xi Jinping and his adoption of more authoritarian policies, suggesting China would have flexed its new-found weight in the world regardless of provocations from the US.

As Hugh White argued in his 2012 book, *The China Choice*, America would have to choose how to respond to China's rise and to the inevitable challenge to its status as the dominant power in a unipolar order. He foresaw that the US-led order did not have long to last. It could try to resist and contain China's rise – a course that he thought would be futile – or find a way to share regional hegemony with China.

As is usual for dominant powers throughout history, the US chose to resist, with seriously adverse implications for Australia's relations with China. Australia did not just follow the US into this policy dead-end, but became a leading champion of it. Gratuitously offending China became a badge of honour in Australian policy circles and among Coalition MPs. It became, as in the Cold War, a test of loyalty. No other country behaved this way or made their relationship with China the barometer of their patriotism.

As Xi set aside the decades-old guidance from Deng Xiaoping – "hide one's strength, bide one's time" – in favour of a more assertive, muscular foreign policy, his signature initiative, the BRI, became the organising principle for China's dealing with states. The US rejected this and Australia followed suit. Security circles in both Washington and Canberra continue to see the BRI as an attempt to impose a China-centric order on the world that had to be resisted. The multipolar order was rapidly taking shape.

Dual orders emerge

In the five years leading up to Russia's invasion of Ukraine, the US increasingly contested China's rise through restrictions and scrutiny of their actions across the spectrum of trade, investment, technology transfer, infrastructure (does anyone remember the Blue Dot initiative?), cyber, outer space and, of course, military. China, for its part, also challenged America.

Before the COVID-19 pandemic, which, to the shock of many Western politicians, revealed the depth of industrial linkages in global supply chains, the Trump administration was advocating "decoupling". This reached a crescendo when the extent of the West's dependency on China for surgical masks and other equipment suddenly became apparent. Domestic concerns were turning politicians against globalisation. This was no less true in Australia under the Morrison government than in Trump's America, despite the fact that Australia had been a major beneficiary, and hence champion, of globalisation.

China's position on decoupling was: "bring it on". Xi Jinping's policy of "dual circulation" was adopted formally in May 2020 but had been under discussion for some time. Effectively it restated the primacy of self-reliance and import substitution. Decoupling would also reduce China's dependence on the West and exposure to moralising on human rights. A key element in the US's position was technological and scientific competition, and accordingly China began massively expanding its investment in knowledge-based industries.

Decoupling fed into Xi's hardening anti-Western narrative. This moved beyond the familiar "century of humiliation" at the hands of foreign occupiers and presented a US-led grand strategy to keep China down, deny proper recognition of its achievements over the past thirty years, and deny the party-state a place as a legitimate leader of world affairs. China was to be second to America, if not subservient. The anti-Western narrative was heightened following COVID and has become a defining aspect of Xi's rule.

The overconfidence and hubris of China's leaders during this time found expression in "wolf warrior" diplomacy, where Chinese diplomats, led by their minister, Wang Yi, seemed to go out of their way to offend and belittle foreign officials or media who dared to criticise China. Wolf warrior diplomacy may be attributed as much to the pervasive influence of social media in China as to deliberate policy choices, especially as the official media has become more tightly controlled. Xi's anti-Western narrative, however, has created a conducive context for aggressive diplomacy, and rampant nationalism on the internet. Both were allowed to run without check and fed off each other.

During 2022, wolf warrior diplomacy has been replaced by more acceptable diplomatic language and behaviour, though considerable damage to China's foreign relations has been done, especially among Western governments and public opinion. The Lowy Institute's 2022 poll found that public trust in Australia towards China has fallen to 12 per cent, from 52 per cent in 2018. No matter what China does, it is likely to take a generation for these attitudes to shift, if they can be shifted at all.

Possibly the biggest negative impact has been in Europe. Previously, most European states endeavoured to maintain positive relations with China while avoiding being drawn into the developing China–US rivalry. That has now changed. The European Union and most member states warn of the dangers of becoming too close to China and of the threat China poses to open democratic societies. In 2020 the European Union, for the first time, classified China as a risk to European values and liberal political systems. In June 2022 at the Madrid NATO summit, China was mentioned for the first time in NATO's revised security assessment. It was described as a "systemic competitor" that challenged NATO's "interests, security and values".

The re-evaluation of Western relationships with China has coincided with the passing of the Trump administration. The Biden administration has sought to restore relations across both the Atlantic and the Pacific, which were badly damaged under Trump, including with NATO, and has bolstered ties with India, Japan, South Korea and

Australia. The administration has also sought to alter regional partnerships, such as the Quad, and has supported the ill-conceived AUKUS security arrangement. The latter is a curious anachronistic grouping of three Anglophone countries. It is unclear what the UK, now searching for relevance post-Brexit, can bring to East Asian security.

For domestic political reasons, US trade arrangements continue to be a lacuna in all this active diplomacy. The Biden administration has continued Trump's policy of not joining the Trans-Pacific Partnership (TPP-11), and undermining the WTO's effectiveness. Meanwhile, China has worked with regional countries to strengthen trade arrangements, such as the Regional Comprehensive Economic Partnership (RCEP), and has applied to join TPP-11, something which Australia is resisting, no doubt at the behest of the US.

Arch realist international theorist John Mearsheimer believes military conflict between the US and China is the most likely outcome from the massive and rapid power shift that has occurred from the US to China. He does, however, concede that war is not inevitable and that a degree of equilibrium in a multipolar world could be based on what he terms "bounded" orders. A bounded order consists of shared values, norms, institutions, trade and investment flows that lead to countries coalescing around a dominant central power. One of these is the US and, of course, the other is China. In a world of "bounded" orders, the leading powers are sometimes in competition with each other and at other times cooperate.

Since the mid-2000s, China has been fashioning an order that reflects its weight in the world. It is not seeking to replace existing institutions it views as serving its own interests, or where prospects exist for them to be shaped to its advantage. China actively participates in UN bodies and is the biggest contributor to UN peacekeeping. It continues to seek a bigger role in the IMF and World Bank, supports the G20, is active within the WTO, APEC and RCEP, and wishes to accede to TPP-11.

At the same time, it has demonstrated considerable institutional entrepreneurship in building and strengthening relations that place it at the centre of networks of countries, giving shape and substance to its leadership of its bounded order. Examples of this activity include the Shanghai Cooperation Organisation, the BRICS grouping (with Brazil, Russia, India and South Africa), which concluded a summit in July, the New Development Bank (previously the BRICS bank), and the Eastern European 17+1 (although this is coming under strain over Lithuania's stance on Taiwan and unhappiness in some countries over China's failure to condemn Russia's invasion of Ukraine). Less formally, China has convened regular summits of African states and in Latin America under the auspice of the China-CELAC Forum.

In the bounded world order that had emerged, the biggest question was how and where did Russia fit

Following Xi Jinping's speech in Astana, Kazakhstan, in 2013, the BRI has developed as the main organising principle of China's bounded order, which was initially a means to ease China's vulnerability on the Strait of Malacca and the South China Sea by opening alternative transport routes for energy and some raw materials. The BRI's activities extend well beyond its original design, and beyond even its main activities involving trade, investment and financing, to include rule making and developing standards – particularly important in telecommunications, where China is the main supplier across all of Eurasia and much of the developing world.

Xi banks on Putin

In the bounded world order that had emerged, the biggest question was how and where did Russia fit. China is now the dominant power in Central Asia and has been extending this influence across Eurasia. Russia's brief but effective military intervention in the threatened uprising against the Kazakhstani government in January 2020 shocked Beijing. It showed that Russia was still prepared to intervene in Eurasia, as it had in Georgia in 2008 and Crimea in 2014, regardless of China's concerns and its principle of non-interference.

Following the West's withdrawal from Afghanistan in August 2021, it seemed that Eurasia would, over time, be dominated by China. Once again, China moved quickly to put itself at the centre of a group of states – Iran, Russia, Pakistan, Turkey – that intended to oversee Afghan security and manage risks of Islamic fundamentalism spreading across Central Asia from Taliban-controlled Afghanistan.

The China–Russia joint statement in February 2022, just twenty days before the Russian invasion of Ukraine, had the flavour of the Molotov–Ribbentrop Pact of August 1939 – a concert of convenience between two powers that understood that conflict between them would be inevitable. In the West, the Xi–Putin statement has been widely misinterpreted. The surprise and dismay with which their statement has been met overlooks the fact that China and Russia, like Nazi Germany and the Soviet Union, are strategic competitors. Putin was most likely looking to ensure that China would somehow be made complicit to his criminality in Ukraine.

It is also unlikely that Putin confided in Xi on his plans to invade. Their joint statement fits neatly with Xi's anti-Western narrative, which has become much sharper in the run-up to this year's crucial 20th Party Congress. The new close relationship with Russia, and the superficial personal rapport between its leaders, would have been seen as a big plus for Xi domestically.

China also wants to be seen as first among equals

The eye-catching headline statement that China–Russia friendship knew "no limits" was presented in China as a great diplomatic achievement for Xi. It meant the existential threat that Russia has always posed to China had been postponed to the indefinite future, allowing China more time to consolidate and extend its dominance over Central Asia and ultimately its power over Russia.

That was until 24 February. The invasion was a disaster for Xi. China was forced to choose between its newly minted special relationship with Russia and the cornerstone of its foreign policy, non-interference.

To complicate matters further, China also had a rare security pact with Ukraine and a special relationship with Kyiv, with substantial commercial underpinnings. Xi's failure to condemn the invasion unequivocally also brought China into direct conflict with a more united and purposeful West.

Xi's flirtation with Putin, and their shared anti-Western stance, meant that China missed an historic opportunity to reset relations with the West post-Trump and post the first wave of COVID. Although Xi's stance appealed to populist sentiment in China, many in China's political elite would have seen this as a major miscalculation. At the National People's Congress, in 2018, when Xi removed fixed terms for presidents, elites felt that he caused China to lose face internationally. China no longer had an agreed institutional mechanism for transferring power and was effectively a personal dictatorship. It was seen as a backward step in China's development. Similarly, by not criticising Russia's invasion, Xi aligned China with a renegade state. The elites in Beijing view China as being better than that. Xi again made the country lose face.

Xi's tacit support of Putin brings to the fore deep tension in China's domestic politics. While the anti-Western narrative plays out well for emphasising China's material success, independence and – most importantly – the respect it has earnt, when it comes to the advanced countries of the world, China also wants to be seen as first among equals.

The rest respond

Xi, like Putin, would have been alarmed at the solidarity, sense of purpose and determination the West found following the invasion. Putin's calculation included a divided and weak response from the West. European states had long accommodated his malicious behaviour, from poisoning adversaries on foreign soil, to Russia's aggression in Georgia, Crimea and eastern Ukraine. US leadership internationally was in tatters following the Trump years, and the country was divided. Fleeing from Afghanistan would also have encouraged Putin to believe that the US was exhausted, as the Soviet Union itself had been when it left Afghanistan. As Putin was amassing troops on the Ukraine border, the West was acrimoniously at odds over the Afghanistan debacle.

The speed, coordination and forcefulness of the West's response would have dismayed Xi. It has been argued that the West could have done more and sooner, short of direct conflict. Even so, the energy and financial sanctions demonstrated that the West was prepared to bear substantial costs to harm the aggressor in defence of basic international norms.

For China's leadership this is especially alarming as it is much more deeply integrated in the international economic system than Russia, from trade and investment flows, holding of foreign government bonds, integration of global supply chains, to elite family fortunes stashed overseas, families resident in the West, reliance on Western education and research, and much more. Unlike Russia, China also faces a significant strategic vulnerability. Among other things, it is the world's biggest importer of crude oil, liquefied natural gas (LNG) and iron ore. Most of this is shipped via the Strait of Malacca – one of the world's most vulnerable transport choke points – and the South China Sea. A concerted effort by the West to block these transport routes would, in a heartbeat, deny China access to the raw materials and energy it needs and bring its economy to its knees.

So, China's failure to condemn the invasion of Ukraine, and the West's preparedness to act collectively, presents China with massive risks and dangers. Already the US has begun to identify and punish Chinese firms that are found to be contributing, albeit indirectly, to Russia's war effort. At its Madrid summit – where NATO classified China as a strategic challenge to its security and values – it was careful to distinguish China from Russia by not naming it as an adversary. However, NATO now believes it has entered an era of competition with China over nuclear arms build-up, and China's bullying of its neighbours, including Taiwan.

Beijing will also be paying close attention to what all this means for any military strike it might launch against Taiwan. An attempted takeover of the island has always been a hypothetical option for Beijing, especially as it explicitly acknowledges that it is prepared to use force. But the probability of China exercising a military option must be regarded as very low. The prospect of success is remote, the question of how to pacify an island of 24 million angry people unresolved, and the threat of effective international retaliation real.

While the war in Ukraine is ongoing and its resolution unknown, Russia's efforts to occupy and subdue a contingent independent territory highlight the extreme difficulty of the task. The likelihood of victory would be much lower in China's case with a sea of some 160 kilometres separating it from its target.

While Putin's threat of first strike use of nuclear weapons may be seen in Beijing as having been successful in staving off direct intervention by NATO, China is much too exposed to Western trade blockades and other sanctions to resort to the military option. Put simply, the costs to China are far too high and the war in Ukraine has shown that such actions can stiffen the West's resolve. Yet, while the lessons for Beijing from Russia's troubled invasion of Ukraine make military options for taking Taiwan much less likely, the weakening overall of Russia through overreach and sanctions strengthens China's position across Eurasia.

[Albanese] may even have hardened the government's position on China

Australia calls in the cavalry

Australia attended the Madrid NATO summit along with other guests from the Asia-Pacific, including Japan, South Korea and New Zealand. The Australian prime minister, Anthony Albanese, said that growing ties between Russia and China posed a "threat to all democratic nations" and drew a parallel between Russia's purported desire to re-establish its empire and China's efforts to win friends and gain influence in the Indo-Pacific. China and Russia were explicitly linked as threats that need to be resisted.

With closer apparent relations between Russia and China, a school of thought – which has found support in the White House – has emerged that there is a single theatre of strategic competition: liberal democracies versus autocracies. It is easy to see the appeal of this formulation, in its simplicity. But viewing the world order as a struggle between might and right, without acknowledging the nuances and subtleties between different countries, runs the risk of increasing the chances of conflict.

It has taken the invasion of Ukraine for policymakers and commentators to take seriously the extent to which the world order has changed. Forty UN members either voted against or abstained on the resolution of 2 March condemning Russia's invasion. Among those that abstained were India and China. Democracies such as Brazil, Argentina, Mexico and, in Australia's region, Indonesia and most of ASEAN failed to join the US in condemning the invasion.

Since 2017, if not earlier, Australia has ever more closely aligned itself with the United States in the US's struggle with China to retain global dominance. Canberra previously sought to fudge the shift from cooperation with China to competition because of China's enormous economic importance, but its strategic policy has become clear and specific. For this, Australia has been rewarded by the US through deeper interoperability between the armed forces, intelligence sharing and most recently the promise of nuclear-powered submarines under the AUKUS arrangement.

In Opposition, Labor supported the government in this shift to competition with China, even if it did so more out of opportunistic political motives than conviction. While acknowledging that Australia and China have substantive differences, Labor seemed to think that the collapse in the relationship was largely about language and tone. It has taken this stance into government. The prime minister's comments at the Madrid NATO summit suggest he now understands that the issues that so deeply divide Australia and China are indeed about substance. Consequently, he may even have hardened the government's position on China.

Senior policy advisers to the government persist with applying the balm that China has changed, not Australia, and that until China becomes more like us, the current state of the relationship is preferable. In short, no government in Canberra, at least for the foreseeable future, has the domestic space in which it can make tangible steps towards an improved relationship with Beijing. Without Russia's invasion of Ukraine, Canberra and Beijing may have been able to find some greater accommodation of each other's positions. China had an opportunity to reset relations with the West, especially Australia, had it condemned the invasion. It chose not to do so. The shape of the new bounded world order is rapidly becoming manifest.

A new world order

A NATO second theatre in Asia, let alone a Biden single global theatre of contest between democracy and autocracy, is a reckless ambition. It would obliterate the UN's founding principle of collective security. It would reinstate conflict between blocs of security arrangements, and encourage states targeted by such blocs to seek similar arrangements. It would make the world a much more dangerous place.

Australia's foreign and security policy is now based on the untested assumption that China is an existential threat. Europe does not see China in the same way. The NATO secretary general made that abundantly clear in his statement at Madrid, as did the prime ministers of Belgium and the Netherlands. Australia seems to have leapt to the conclusion that Russia and China are one and the same and pose the same threats. Europe has not. It will not allow Asia to become a second NATO theatre.

It is wishful thinking by Australian politicians to believe that the US still has the political will to lead the West in a second theatre in Asia. As America has sought to push back against China, it has itself become domestically more divided. This is likely to become more pronounced during the midterm elections, which could see Democrats in a minority in the House, and Washington even more gridlocked. The next US presidential election is full of great uncertainties. In these circumstances, it is strategic folly to have so comprehensively glued Australia to the hip of the US in its confrontation with China.

It is also fanciful to assume that the old order can be restored. The most desirable order would be one based on rules that reflect the values of liberal democracies. But that era, to the extent it ever really existed, has long passed.

The international system has not yet, however, returned to the state of anarchy to which it has always had a tendency. Until the invasion of Ukraine, US military pre-eminence was believed to underpin the stability of the international system. This is no longer the case. The rise of China, while it has upended the old order, also brings a new form of order and stability. Its markets and investment flows support economic growth in much of the developing world. It builds infrastructure, with little hard evidence of a nefarious debt-diplomacy agenda, despite the claims of critics. It has put in place multilateral arrangements which seem to work well enough and attract support. Whether we like it or not, and usually we don't, it offers developing countries an alternative paradigm to that of the US-dominated West. China's bounded order is now well established and includes nearly all of Australia's regional neighbours as well as much of the Pacific. Unless there is a catastrophe in China, which would add to instability in the region and might also threaten Australia's security, China and its order are not going away.

In the new order, Australia must make its peace with China

If Russia is defeated and humiliated in Ukraine, China will be the unchallenged power across Eurasia. If Russia prevails, China and Russia will draw closer for a time to challenge the international liberal order. In any event, China's global influence will only be strengthened. In the long term, China's and Russia's interests are likely to collide as they compete for Central Asia to ensure their own security. Australia inevitably faces a vastly and permanently altered security landscape.

It is one which is so unfamiliar that Australian policymakers are still struggling to recognise it.

Australia has had the luxury of the global dominant power sharing our values, if not always our interests, and we have felt secure in the belief that we have great and powerful friends to stand by us. Of course, that was not the case when put to the test in 1942, when Britain abandoned Australia, understandably enough, to defend its own interests. Today, it would be dangerous folly to assume that America will always be there for us, or that the US will have either the will or the capacity to prevail in any conflict against China.

In the new order, Australia must make its peace with China. Of course, this has to be on terms that do not compromise Australia's interests. Australia needs then to decide if its foreign and security policies will continue to be based on siding with the US in its rivalry with China, or whether it will recognise the reality of Chinese power and influence in the region and seek ways to work with China to promote stability and peace. Australia has foreign policy options other than the US–China binary. It is time for these to be explored.

Australia in the past has demonstrated considerable skill and flair in working with regional neighbours and beyond to build coalitions to advance its interests. It created the Cairns Group, which changed agricultural trade rules globally; it formed APEC; it initiated the Canberra Commission on nuclear disarmament; it led, with Indonesia, the resolution of the Cambodian conflict; it had the courage to stand against unreasonable US demands for IMF conditionality on Indonesia during the Asian financial crisis; for a time it led a group of developing and emerging economies to reform the IMF to reflect the growth of East Asia; it established, with Indonesia, the regional forum on people smuggling, and much more.

Australia should be working with ASEAN neighbours on developing security mechanisms aimed at increasing habits of consultation and building trust in the region, not, as we do now, seeking to stoke tensions. With its neighbours, Australia should be promoting nuclear weapons controls and disarmament in Asia. It should be active, through coalitions, in reminding China that bad behaviour will carry costs. On a more constructive note, Australia as the region's biggest energy exporter and China as the world's biggest energy importer should be able to put together a plan to advance regional energy security and sustainability.

The challenge for Australian foreign and security policy is to deal with the world as it is, not as we might wish it to be. This will require a return not only to a central role for an elevated diplomatic effort, but investment in the skills that underpin that, including language, history and cultural studies. If the past year has taught us anything, it is that in international affairs there is no sensible centre, just interests and power, egos and ambition.

The future agenda for Australia is big and urgent. ■

TOUGH TIMES

Securing Australia's trade in an era of upheaval

Jeffrey Wilson

International trade should be boring. Like the water supply, or trains running on time, trade is taken for granted and largely unnoticed until something goes wrong. This is a good thing. It is the result of decades of effort to build an open and rules-based global trade system, which allows countries to predictably trade with each other for mutual benefit. When we don't hear about trade, we know the system is working.

So it is rather worrying to see trade make a dramatic return to the headlines. Trade wars between the US and China. Multi-billion-dollar sanctions against Russia. The WTO descending into crisis. Global supply chains seizing up. Protectionist backlashes and economic decoupling. Chronic shortages of essential goods. The end of globalisation? Trade is interesting again, for all the wrong reasons.

The crisis in the global trade system is a significant – though widely under-appreciated – challenge for Australia. Ours is an open economy, which since the 1970s has relied on trade with Indo-Pacific partners as a driver of national wealth. We have developed world-class export industries in commodities and services, while sourcing critical inputs from efficient global supply chains. This open trade strategy allows us to exploit our comparative advantages and share in the economic dynamism of the Indo-Pacific.

But our trade openness relies on a permissive external environment. For three decades, the global trade system has provided it. We could successfully reorient our economy to new trade opportunities in our region – sometimes with politically challenging partners – because the rules-based system offered protection against political risks. However, as the integrity of this system breaks down, Australia finds itself alone. In the last five years, Australian businesses have had to contend with Trump's trade wars, Chinese economic coercion, a supply chain crisis and an energy crisis resulting from Russia's invasion of Ukraine. Gone are the days when we could trade in the confidence that geopolitical shocks would not derail our economic connections to the world.

Australia cannot change the geopolitical currents that are threatening the global trade system. But nor can we give up on openness. Trade is too important to our prosperity to ignore or abandon. So we must prepare ourselves for the challenge, by ensuring that our trade outlook is configured to the geopolitical reality we now face.

The road ahead will prove difficult. Australia needs to rethink the fundamental principles that have enabled us to make trade a core part of our economic success for a generation. But it can be done.

Beating our trade ploughshares back into swords

History will not remember Donald Trump for his clarity or consistency. But on one issue – hostility to trade and the international institutions that govern it – his presidency delivered exactly what it promised. Trump's stated trade philosophy was remarkably succinct: "Trade wars are good, and easy to win." He campaigned on an economic platform largely defined by anti-trade sentiment. Upon assuming the presidency, he quickly began using the "trade weapon" as a foreign policy tool – in his first week in office he signed an executive order to withdraw from the Trans-Pacific Partnership (TPP), a twelve-member "mega-regional" FTA negotiated during the Obama administration. Under the threat of punitive tariffs, Japan, Korea, Canada and Mexico were forced to negotiate agreements that would see them buy more American goods. Steel and aluminium tariffs were applied worldwide on dubious "national security" grounds. Appointments to the WTO's Appellate Body were vetoed, preventing the global trade umpire from hearing appeals.

The coup de grâce was a trade war launched against China in 2018. Initially Chinese steel and aluminium were targeted, but the two countries were drawn into a cycle of tit-for-tat retaliation, which ultimately saw tariffs applied to nearly half a trillion dollars of bilateral trade. A ceasefire was reached in late 2019, where China agreed to import US$200 billion of additional American products over the next two years. However, the pandemic intervened, China was unable to meet the import commitment, and the deal collapsed. US–China trade ties have been locked in a stalemate since, with neither side willing to lay down its arms.

By declaring a trade war, Trump was breaking a key – if unspoken – rule of the post–Cold War order: not to use trade as a geopolitical weapon. In the 1990s, trade was widely viewed as a vehicle to bridge the divides of the Cold War. An implicit bargain was struck, where trade and geopolitics were kept on separate foreign policy tracks. Thereafter, China, Vietnam and the former Soviet countries were brought into Western economic institutions, such as the WTO, and trade was used to spur their post-communist rebuilding. By bringing East and West together within a common rule framework, trade relationships ceased to be anchored within geopolitical blocs.

China's integration into the global economy – it is now the top trading partner for over 120 countries – shows that governments did not have to be geopolitically aligned to trade with each other. Of course, Trump was not alone in tearing up the post–Cold War trade rulebook. China had been politicising trade for nearly a decade. It began in 2010, when it banned rare-earth exports to Japan for two months during a dispute over the contested Senkaku/Diaoyu Islands. In subsequent years, eight other countries have been targeted by similar forms of Chinese trade sanctions (see table over the page).

Target	Commodities affected	Proximate political cause
Japan, 2010	Rare-earth minerals	Contested illegal fishing in East China Sea
Norway, 2011	Salmon	Nobel Committee awarded Peace Prize to Liu Xiaobo
Philippines, 2012	Bananas	Successful litigation action in South China Sea dispute
Mongolia, 2016	Mineral products	Dalai Lama granted visa
Taiwan, 2016	Tourism, education	Tsai Ing-wen elected president
South Korea, 2017	Tourism, automobiles, department stores	Installed anti-ballistic missile system to defend against DPRK missile strikes
Canada, 2019	Canola, soy, pork, beef	Executed arrest warrant in compliance with valid US extradition request
Australia, 2020	Coal, barley, beef, tourism, education, wine, cotton, wheat, wool, lobster, sugar, copper, timber, table grapes	Several perceived foreign policy decisions, culminating in a call for an international inquiry into the origins of COVID-19
Lithuania, 2021	Suspension of rail services and food export licences	Establishment of a "Taiwan Representative Office"

These coercive trade practices leverage one of China's major geopolitical strengths – its massive domestic market – to pressure other countries. The sanction itself might only affect a small volume of goods, functioning as a diplomatic "warning shot" rather than a full-scale trade war, but the objective is to impose political conditions on access to its market, and to warn governments off policies that it dislikes.

Russia's invasion of Ukraine has added yet more fuel to the trade warfare fire. The response by Western allies has been two-pronged: military aid to Ukraine, and economic sanctions against Russia. In the first weeks of the war, Western sanctions targeted Russian banks and individuals with political or business connections to the Kremlin. But as the conflict dragged on, trade bans became a more prominent – and potentially more powerful – tool.

Some sanctions have targeted Russia's export earnings, such as EU and US bans on Russian oil and/or gas. Others have targeted its imports of critical goods, including bans on supplying metals, electronics and advanced manufacturing products. The purpose is to disrupt the Russian economy, and thus diminish its war-fighting ability. Australia, Japan, Switzerland, Korea, Singapore, the UK, the EU and the US have all now imposed trade bans of some kind.

The bicycle theory of liberalisation

Unfortunately, this outbreak of trade warfare comes at the worst possible time for the global open trade system. The pillars that have underpinned this system – the easing of trade barriers, and the rules-based WTO that has negotiated and enforced the opening of markets – have in recent years come under extraordinary strain.

For two decades following the end of the Cold War, trade liberalisation swept the world. Most governments reduced their levels of protection, either unilaterally as part of domestic economic reforms, or as a result of joining the WTO and signing bilateral FTAs. This trend enabled many countries, particularly Australia and our partners in the Indo-Pacific, to rapidly expand their trade.

However, the pendulum has since swung back towards protectionism. Following the global financial crisis, many governments began reimposing trade restrictions. According to data compiled by Global Trade Alert, in the decade to 2021, governments enacted 28,793 policies which are "harmful" to trade, and only 5988 "liberalising" measures – a five-to-one ratio in favour of protectionism. Many of the largest players have jumped on the bandwagon. The US, China, India and EU members account for the lion's share of the global total.

Why has protectionism made a comeback? One explanation is the "bicycle theory" of trade liberalisation. It posits that domestic demands for trade protection are an omnipresent phenomenon, to which governments will inevitably succumb unless some external factor forces them to liberalise. Continually striking new international agreements – which offer economic gains that can forestall demands for protection – is required to stop backsliding. Trade liberalisation is thus akin to riding a bicycle: "if it stops going forwards, it'll fall over."

And indeed, the bicycle has ground to a halt. Since the creation of the WTO in 1995, not a single "negotiating round" – where members agree on a comprehensive package of reforms – has been completed. By contrast, its predecessor – the General Agreement on Tariffs and Trade (GATT) – completed eight rounds over its five-decade history. Negotiations for the Doha Round, the WTO's only attempt at comprehensive negotiations, collapsed in 2008 due to irreconcilable differences between developed and developing countries.

Nor have fallback efforts to strike deals in specific sectors delivered results. Longstanding WTO talks on environmental goods and dispute settlement are in deadlock. Significant divisions remain over emerging issues such as e-commerce and carbon tariffs. Even agreeing to an intellectual property waiver for the manufacture of COVID vaccines took until June 2022 – too late to make a difference during the height of the pandemic.

An explanation for the WTO's lack of progress lies in the achievement viewed as a marker of its success: its global expansion. During the Cold War, the GATT was a tight-knit club of Western countries and friends with a shared commitment to open trade. But with post–Cold War expansion – the WTO now boasts 164 members – its complexion changed dramatically. New members brought to Geneva different developmental levels, economic systems and trade objectives. Yet the WTO's "single undertaking" rule, in which all parties must agree to proposals before they advance, has proven unworkable with a larger and more diverse membership. Expectations for new global-level agreements out of Geneva are extremely low.

Worse still, the WTO's enforcement powers have collapsed. Criticism has been levelled at the WTO's Appellate Body (the equivalent of an appeals court) and its members (akin to judges) for exceeding their official mandate in recent judicial decisions. While many countries have expressed concerns, the US has been most activist in demanding change. Since 2016, the US has vetoed new appointments to the Appellate Body, playing a game of chicken to force others to the negotiating table.

By December 2019, the Appellate Body had become inquorate. Since then, it has been unable to hear new cases referred to it by the dispute settlement mechanism. This has allowed governments to easily evade WTO enforcement through a tactic known as the "appeal into the void" – if you automatically appeal an adverse ruling, the case disappears into an indefinite legal purgatory. Many, including China, India, Korea, the US and the EU, have exploited this tactic. The crisis has left the WTO without a depoliticised and effective enforcement mechanism.

The integrity of an open and rules-based trade system is less assured than at any recent time. Governments are turning back towards protectionism at home, while using trade as a weapon in geopolitical conflicts. These trends are occurring while the global institutions supporting trade have lost their teeth. For open and trade exposed economies like Australia, this new era of barriers and discord demands a rethink of how we economically engage with the world.

A free-trader in a protectionist world

The crisis in the global trade system is a greatly under-appreciated threat to Australia's national interests. Australia is a medium-sized and advanced economy which relies heavily on trade. The nation has a suite of world-leading export industries, drawn from the resources, agriculture, services and advanced manufacturing sectors. Their global competitiveness is, in turn, secured by access to imported goods and technologies.

It was not always thus. For the three decades after World War II, Australia was a committed protectionist. Tariffs were an integral part of the political compromise between capital and labour, known as the post-war "Australian settlement". Unions were protected by centralised wage arbitration and the White Australia policy, and, as compensation, industry was sheltered from international competition behind high tariff walls.

Australia's public call … for an international inquiry into the origins of COVID-19 proved to be the straw that broke the camel's back

But this social compromise was dismantled from the Whitlam government onwards. Protectionism, no longer politically necessary, was recognised as a brake on economic progress. During the 1980s and 1990s, tariffs were gradually removed, the dollar floated and capital markets opened to foreign investors. And then in the 2000s, Australia began enthusiastically negotiating FTAs with all the major economies of the Indo-Pacific. Australia now has seventeen FTAs, covering 82 per cent of our two-way trade.

This free trade play largely worked. First, to paraphrase the Whitlam government's minister for minerals and energy, Rex Connor, Australia moved "off the sheep's back, and into the coal truck" by developing mining export industries to supply the newly industrialising economies of Asia. Technology and service intensive exporters, such as education and digital, soon followed, targeting the region's emerging middle class. Foreign investment flowed in to finance these growing export sectors, bringing new technologies with it.

Within only a generation, Australia had transitioned to a highly open economy tapped into surging Indo-Pacific markets. Our subsequent world-record run of twenty-nine years recession free (1991–2020) is a testament to the success of the open trade strategy.

However, the strategy relied – and still relies – on a permissive external environment. And the breakdown of this permissive environment has taken a toll on Australia, forcing it to contend with a growing list of trade shocks.

Trump's trade wars were the first. Australia was fortunate to escape direct impact. Few industries were affected, and deft diplomacy saw Australia negotiate an exception to Trump's steel tariffs in 2018. But the indirect effects could not be avoided. America's tariffs on Chinese steel and aluminium are inherently an indirect tariff on the Australian iron ore and bauxite used to manufacture them.

We soon faced geopolitical trade shocks head on, when in 2020 Australia was targeted by Chinese economic coercion. The political causes were complex, reflecting a range of irritants. Chinese aggression abroad and foreign interference at home irked Canberra, while Australia's public criticism of China on issues like the South China Sea, Xinjiang and Hong Kong upset Beijing. But Australia's public call in April 2020 for an international inquiry into the origins of COVID-19 proved to be the straw that broke the camel's back.

China responded with an unprecedented campaign of sanctions extending to fifteen sectors. Barley and wine were hit with anti-dumping duties, while Australian coal import quotas were cancelled. Students and tourists were officially warned off travelling to Australia. Many agricultural products – beef, lobster, wheat, sugar and timber – faced "grey zone" sanctions, where Chinese customs authorities arbitrarily banned Australian shipments. Most of Australia's major exports to China were interrupted in some way. Only iron ore was spared, reflecting the dependence of China's steel industry on Australian supplies.

Australia needs a new strategy to succeed as a free-trader in a world of protectionism

Chinese trade sanctions were a terrible political and commercial shock. At the time of the sanctions, China – Australia's top trade partner – accounted for 38 per cent of exports. For industries like lobster, timber and wine, their principal market collapsed overnight. The economic effects were ultimately relatively mild – Treasury estimates suggest only A$1 billion of net export losses – as many of the industries found alternate buyers. But the experience hammered home the reality that Australia could no longer assume its trade was insulated from geopolitical risk.

Russia's invasion of Ukraine has put this reality beyond doubt. Australia rightly joined the Western sanctions, applying 35 per cent tariffs to all Russian products in April this year. The impacts have been limited to the handful of products (mainly fertiliser and steel) the two countries trade. But the effect on global markets has been huge. Between the impacts of invasion itself and subsequent sanctions, prices for food, minerals and energy have exploded. Global value chains, already disrupted by the pandemic, are under even further strain.

The Russian trade shock brought winners and losers. Australia is an exporter of many affected commodities, and primary producers are benefiting from prices at all-time highs. But we are equally a consumer of these same commodities. Wholesale electricity prices doubled in the first quarter of 2022, crimping industrial production and straining household finances. An inflationary breakout in early 2022 was in large part driven by soaring import prices, forcing the Reserve Bank to raise interest rates.

Geopolitical trade shocks have reshaped Australia's economic fortunes. For the first time in a generation, Australia must contend with how geopolitics will affect our connections to the global economy. The success of our free trade pivot from the 1970s was premised on a liberalising and rule-governed trading environment. But as the American, Chinese and Russian shocks have demonstrated, this environment is no longer a given. Australia needs a new strategy to succeed as a free-trader in a world of protectionism.

Friends with trade benefits

There are no easy fixes for countries like Australia. As a middle power, we lack the political weight to meaningfully change global trends towards protectionism. And we are not large enough to sustain a diverse and competitive economy without openness to trade. Yet if we do nothing, these global trends will threaten our economic future.

The question is: How to adapt to an era of politicised trade, without sacrificing the openness on which Australia's wealth is based?

A new "trusted trade" concept may offer a solution. Put simply, it proposes that priority should be accorded to partners whose political attributes mean they are likely to be more reliable. Trusted trade upends the conventional logic of liberalisation, which calls for barriers to be removed so trade follows purely market forces. Instead, we should deliberately cultivate trade with reliable partners, even where these may differ from those we would choose if applying a commercial logic. In an era of geopolitical risk, trade should at least partially "follow the flag".

The attraction of trusted trade is that it avoids throwing the free-trade baby out with the geopolitical bathwater. Countries can remain committed to open trade (the good), but preference partners to minimise political risks (the bad). Trusted trade is already being applied in a variety of creative ways. In the context of global value chains, it manifests in the practice of "friend-shoring". When imports of critical goods are interrupted by politically motivated trade barriers, it is not always viable for businesses to "onshore" production back home. This is especially true of Australia, which lacks the scale to have technical expertise in every possible product we require. Instead, Australia can relocate production to "friendly" countries – defined as those posing fewer risks of political interruptions.

Friend-shoring is already underway through so-called China Plus One corporate strategies. During the US–China trade war, many textile manufacturers shifted final assembly from China to Mexico to avoid Trump's tariffs. In 2022, Apple moved some of its iPad production to Vietnam as a result of interruptions due to China's continuing COVID lockdowns. Ongoing efforts to develop an Australian rare-earths industry – a critical mineral needed for electric vehicles (EVs), in which China holds a global near-monopoly – follow a similar logic.

Trust is even informing to whom we export. Businesses typically focus on their most valuable customers, resulting in dependence on a small number of export markets. If a political event interrupts trade with a major partner, the effects can be dire. Diversification to friends can be an important insurance policy, even if it leads to reduced revenue by trading with less profitable markets.

Sometimes, diversification is forced upon you. In the wake of Chinese sanctions in 2020, affected businesses scrambled to place product in new markets: coal went to India, barley to Saudi Arabia and South-East Asia, copper to Europe and Japan, and cotton to Bangladesh and Vietnam. While these new markets cushioned the blow of Chinese sanctions, they were not without their own costs. Australian commodities usually commanded a price premium in the Chinese market, which had to be foregone with the pivot towards new buyers.

Trust is also reshaping trade diplomacy. As protectionism and trade conflict grows, governments are refocusing their diplomatic efforts on allies and friends. The US and the EU established a Trade and

Technology Council in 2021, aimed to ensure trade would be "informed by national security and scientific priorities as well as by economic and commercial priorities". To lessen its reliance on China, Japan has made agreements with the US and Taiwan to jointly develop the semiconductor industry. Australia's recent FTAs with the UK and India have been officially billed as enabling trade diversification with trusted partners – a clear, if implicit, nod to minimising export dependence on China.

Perhaps the most interesting initiative is the US-led Indo-Pacific Economic Framework (IPEF). Launched in 2022, it is not a conventional trade agreement, but a framework for club-based negotiations on digital trade, supply chains, green technology, and tax and transparency issues. The most telling part of IPEF is its membership: only fourteen US-friendly countries, including Japan, India and Australia, are currently involved, with China notably absent. IPEF is an ongoing initiative, and it remains to be seen where it will land. However, it lays an obvious marker that the future of trade agreements will not be open to all, but only to exclusive clubs negotiated between friends.

This trusted trade world looks nothing like the free-trade world which it is replacing. Market forces are no longer the sole criterion for determining who trades with who. Political calculations cast a shadow over commercial logic, while trade clubs are erected between friendly governments. The integrated global trade system – on which Australia has relied for three decades – is being replaced by a patchwork of politically mediated trade blocs. How does Australia navigate this new environment?

Australia's trusted trade future

Australia's current trade outlook was developed in the free-trade era of the 1990s and proved very successful in that environment. But we will need new settings configured to a less-reliable global trading system. Fortunately, the process of adapting is less daunting than it may seem.

Our relationship with China is the largest and most immediate concern. For two years, China has waged a concerted campaign of trade coercion against Australia. While the election of the Albanese government in May has lowered the diplomatic temperature, a return to the past is extremely unlikely. China has now deployed coercion against nine countries – subsequently to us, against Lithuania in 2021 – and shows no sign of shelving the tactic. We must be alert to the possibility that the next geopolitical crisis will again disrupt the China trade relationship.

However, there are alternatives. Australia is geographically blessed to be in the Indo-Pacific, a region replete with some of the world's largest and fastest-growing economies. Japan and Korea are well-established trade partners; Indonesia and Vietnam are rapidly advancing to middle-income status; and India will soon emerge as an economic giant. While none of these partners matches the size of China, together they make a formidable bloc.

Equally importantly, Australia has good political ties with all. The India relationship has advanced over the last decade and was capped in April by the signing of a bilateral FTA – India's first comprehensive FTA in many years. Japan is a longstanding partner, and the economic relationship was recently augmented by a reciprocal access agreement for defence – Japan's first security agreement with a country beside the US. Japan and India are participants in the Quad, while South Korea, Indonesia and Vietnam have also signed on to the US-led IPEF process. A potential "trusted trade" network already exists on Australia's doorstep. The question is how to turn it into reality.

To diversify partners, Australia will need to diversify the kinds of trade we do. Dependence on China is not an accident, but a natural consequence of our commodity-focused trade profile. Others simply don't need Australia's iron ore, coal, gas, wheat and beef in the volumes that China does. Fostering a broader base of export industries is the only way to bring more trusted partners into the mix. Fortunately, there are many attractive options ready to go.

Trusted trade is a prudent insurance policy in an uncertain and contested world

The energy transition provides immediate opportunities. While Australia is currently a hydrocarbon exporter, it is extremely well-endowed in critical minerals (such as lithium, cobalt and rare earths) required for renewable energy systems. It is already a major player in some of these sectors, and as the energy transition gathers pace global demand will soar. The automotive industry – which is well-established in Japan and Korea and growing in India – will be a huge potential critical minerals market as EVs become the dominant transport technology.

Longer-term, green hydrogen – an energy commodity like gas, but made with renewables – provides a useful complement. Hydrogen is an emerging but revolutionary technology, as it enables clean energy trade between renewables-rich producers like Australia to renewables-poor consumers in Asia. The net-zero transition plans of many partners, particularly Japan and Korea, already factor in a large supply of green hydrogen from the 2030s. And Australia is the only country in the region that can realistically supply the volumes required. Our existing gas trade with Northeast Asia provides a commercial foundation on which the infrastructure for green hydrogen exports can be built.

India opens new opportunities in technology. It is committed to manufacturing being a large component of its future economy, as part of the Modi government's *Atmanirbhar Bharat* ("self-reliant India") concept. But while India possesses the labour resources for a globally competitive manufacturing sector, this will need to be supported by imports in high-technology niches. Australia's knowledge-intensive economy is a perfect complement. Indian companies have already telegraphed a strong interest in Australia's advanced manufacturing, resource processing, engineering and digital tech sectors.

These new trusted trade opportunities are all aligned to Australia's commercial strengths, and exploit our competitive niche in the global economy. They are future-oriented sectors with considerable room for growth. They also provide Australia a way to "climate-proof" our trade profile, by gradually transitioning from carbon-intensive commodities to the products needed for climate adaptation. But to build these industries, we will need to invest in new trade, investment and technology partnerships. Our economic and commercial diplomacy should be reoriented towards trusted partners.

And they make good geopolitical sense. Australia has strong relationships with these partners, who largely "sit on the same side of the fence" as us when it comes to the main cleavages shaping the world today. While trade shocks like those from Trump, China and Russia can never be ruled out, they are less likely to happen with these partners, and in these new industries. Trusted trade is a prudent insurance policy in an uncertain and contested world.

Of course, this is not a binary choice. Building a green hydrogen trade with Japan, or advanced manufacturing with India, does not mean exiting the commodity trade with China. Both China and the resource sector are far too important to Australia to abandon. But it does mean thinking about what we can do now to ensure our economic role in the world is future-proofed against geopolitical conflict. Building these trusted relationships is an investment in a more secure economic future.

It won't be easy, but we have to do it. Australia has had a good run with the open and rules-based global trade system. When the geopolitical winds changed for the better at the end of the Cold War, we quickly pivoted to open trade and benefited immensely. With these winds now changing for worse, trusted trade relationships will allow us to thrive in tough times. ■

TURNING POINT

Can Europe be a strong global power?

Laura Tingle

The elevated part of the Friedrichstraße train station in Berlin, all grime and steel, is an architectural homage to the industrial age. It feels like you should only ever see pictures of it in black and white. This is, in fact, often the case, because it became most famous during the Cold War, brooding next to the eastern bank of the river Spree – the major border crossing between East and West Berlin.

Sitting next to, and overshadowed by, the station is a rather dingy faded blue building: one of the gaudy parts of what is the historically complex and mawkish Berlin tourist trail. From 1962 until 1989, this building served as the crossing point between East and West, known as the *Tränenpalast*, or "Palace of Tears".

We start our journey into the state of European – and particularly German – foreign and defence policy, circa 2022, at Friedrichstraße because of a storefront that opened on the other side of the station from the Palace of Tears eight years ago. It is a recruitment office for the Bundeswehr, the German armed forces. When the office opened, it was presided over by then defence minister Ursula von der Leyen, who is now the president of the European Commission.

A German friend points it out to me one day as we leave the station, recounting what a radical thing it was at the time: a striking shift after seventy years of Germans' discomfort with being seen to be promoting militarism or anything associated with it. And here it is, sitting smack bang amid all these other symbols of the European struggles of war, division, power and ideas. The office was supposed not just to sign up recruits but also to persuade people of the great opportunities for employment that the Bundeswehr represented.

You cannot underestimate how World War II – and the trouble modern Germans have in understanding how their society produced and supported the Nazis – permeates so much here. Strategists will explain, for example, that Germany's approach to Russia, which seems to have long been inexplicably soft, was due to what Germany did to Russians during the war. But it is also reflected in aspects of the way the German state operates. For example, Germany has only recently started to develop a national security strategy. It has no equivalent of a national security committee of cabinet. There is a hot debate about how the institutions that run foreign policy and aid coordinate what they do.

Policy analyst Gudrun Wacker, who works at Stiftung Wissenschaft und Politik – the German Institute for International and

Security Affairs (SWP) – told me: "It's always difficult to use the word strategy in relation to German foreign policy, because, first of all, until a few years ago, we didn't even speak about having national interests. We spoke about values. We had norms and standards but pretended not to have national interests."

For more than a decade Christoph Heusgen was Angela Merkel's most senior foreign policy adviser. He then served as Germany's ambassador to the United Nations and now heads the Munich Security Conference – the European version of the Shangri-La Dialogues. He argues that if Germany had "a proper National Security Council" it would have considered issues like energy security: the extent of its reliance on Russia for gas; its lack of gas storage facilities; who owned those facilities; and how Russia was shifting its delivery of gas from 2021 onwards.

But back to the railway station recruitment office, which would have to be counted as a dismal failure. There's a lot of history to overcome, of course. Those shadows of world war are long and haunt the country's politics and the awkward national discussion about what Germany's own defence needs are – and its role in European defence – as well as German society.

In the intervening years, the Bundeswehr has struggled to boost – or even maintain – its numbers. In early 2019, the *Financial Times* was reporting that "just 20,000 recruits joined the armed forces in 2018, down from 23,000 the previous year, and the lowest in the history of the Bundeswehr". At the boots-on-the-ground level, the military was just not cool. In a booming and prosperous German economy, why would you bother seeking a career there? And just as it is hard to underestimate how pervasive the echoes of history are in German politics, it's hard to overstate the ambivalence of Germans and their politicians to the military and spending.

In 2011, after the global financial crisis, Angela Merkel instigated spending cuts for defence. At the same time, compulsory conscription was suspended and limits were put on the number of military bases. In 2014, the Bundeswehr acknowledged the German armed forces had such chronic equipment problems that it rendered them "unable to deliver its defensive NATO promises". Most of its fighter aircraft were out of action.

But after Russia's annexation of Crimea in March 2014, this started to turn around.

In 2015, there was an announcement of an increase in defence spending and talk of fully modernising the army. Spending was further increased over the following couple of years, though not enough to even begin to appease the criticism from a series of US administrations that Germany was the lead culprit among European members of NATO that were not doing their fair share of spending.

These tensions – legitimate at their core – boiled over at the drama-filled NATO meeting in London in 2019.

That was the meeting where US president Donald Trump and British prime minister Boris Johnson did not meet because of concerns about Trump's interference in the looming UK election, and where Trump called Canada "slightly delinquent" in its contribution to

NATO. Trump also clashed with Emmanuel Macron, the young French president ambitious and impatient to develop a long-term European security strategy.

But for the purpose of this piece, it was the rift between Macron and Merkel that was the most significant. Macron, who was growing increasingly frustrated by Germany's slow pace of action – and Merkel's caution – called the alliance "brain dead", prompting uncharacteristic anger from Merkel, who was reported as telling him: "I understand your desire for disruptive politics. But I'm tired of picking up the pieces. Over and over, I have to glue together the cups you have broken so that we can then sit down and have a cup of tea together."

The great irony – given the way events have unfolded in 2022 – is that Macron's problem reflected the forces then at play within German domestic politics: the left-leaning Social Democrats were resisting his European military and security proposals, and Merkel's conservative Christian Democrats were blocking his proposals for more economic integration, higher spending and eurozone reform.

So here is a thread of a broader European story in 2022: it's not just that Germany is made cautious by its history and was lulled into a false sense of security by recent decades of peace, it's that the very story of its economic success means that, even today, months after Vladimir Putin shocked the world in Ukraine, there is a strange sense of lethargy in Germany about what that means and what needs to be done about it.

Germany is not everything in Europe. But as the region's economic superpower, and with its modern history of reluctant leadership, any metamorphosis it makes towards a role of strategic leadership will reshape the future of Europe. The widening membership of both NATO and the EU suggests policy should not, and will not, simply be led and shaped by those two powers.

But Germany and France – the latter being the only continental nuclear power in Western Europe – remain the behemoths around which others, for now at least, move. And they have very different perceptions of their strategic positions: Germany remains steadfastly of the view that European security must rest on the United States – much as Australia sees its security in its own region, particularly in the face of the rise of China. That might not be all that surprising given the historical presence of US troops in Germany, even if it is down from around a quarter of a million at the time of the fall of the Berlin Wall to just over 35,000 in September last year.

Macron's vision – of a European defence strategy – remains one that is regularly criticised

But France – especially under Macron – sees the world differently. Macron wants Europe to develop its own defence strategy – a long-held belief that was reinforced by the announcement of the AUKUS deal in September last year. The AUKUS announcement didn't just disrupt Australia's relationship with France. Macron withdrew the French ambassador to Washington for a time and he observed that Europeans had to "come out of their naivete" on the world stage and assert their independence from the United States.

"For a bit over ten years now, the United States has been very focused on itself and has strategic interests that are being reoriented towards China and the Pacific," he said. "It's in their right to do so," he continued, but "we would be naive, or rather we would make a terrible mistake, to not want to draw the consequences."

Things were subsequently smoothed over when Macron and US president Joe Biden said in a joint statement that the United States "recognises the importance of a stronger and more capable European defence". For his part, Macron said the United States was "a great historical ally and an ally in terms of values. And that'll remain the case".

A greater European emphasis on its own defence would not constitute an "alternative to our alliance with the United States", he said, adding that it would happen "within the framework of NATO".

Macron's vision – of a European defence strategy – remains one that is regularly criticised for being too vague and too focused on reinforcing French leadership (given its status as the only nuclear power in the grouping).

Something else is different about the way France and Germany see the world.

In Germany, priority is given to geoeconomics over geopolitics – it wants to keep its economy afloat first and to think about geopolitics and strategy second. Even now, it is seen as giving at least an equal role to the economic consequences of Russia's move into Ukraine as the defence implications.

At the time of writing, the outcome of the war in Ukraine is unclear.

This essay reflects the views gathered in interviews conducted in Europe in July and tries to give an insight into the mindset there – and the extent to which it is changing.

And the striking thing at that time was the overriding presence – just as Europe envisages a radical redefinition characterised by boldness and strength – of lethargy.

It's not that there have not been attempts to shake off the lethargy, even before Ukraine.

In 2017, Macron shocked the French establishment by almost wiping out the traditional political parties to win the presidency and dominate the parliament with his En Marche! movement. He has a Napoleonic intellectual and strategic busyness – some would say ambition – to him. And he is avowedly European. Among the barrage of work he demanded from a galvanised French bureaucracy in 2017 was the rapid drafting of a new white paper on security and defence which aimed to have France take the lead on European defence policy.

"The Europe of today is too weak, too slow, too inefficient"

Another notable part of the strategic review, to Australian eyes, was much blunter language than we were using at the time about China. And the paper did not just see China as a geostrategic risk in the Indo-Pacific. France had concerns about the critical infrastructure investments across Europe. Its historical interests in Africa made it acutely aware of China's influence across that continent too. And it had a sophisticated view of the Indo-Pacific – including the need to keep sea lanes open in the Pacific – that extended beyond the protection of citizens in its Pacific territories.

These concerns were matched by alarm that China now controls the place where every significant submarine communications cable makes landfall – Djibouti. It now also owns and controls one of the largest shipping ports in Europe: Piraeus, just outside Athens.

Macron followed up the release of the strategic review with a (very) long, nationally televised speech given at the Sorbonne. "I have come to talk to you about Europe," he began. "'Again?!' some might exclaim. People will just have to get used to it, because I will not stop talking about it. Because this is where our battle lies, our history, our identity, our horizon, what protects us and gives us a future."

Macron told his audience:

> It is up to us, to you, to map out the route which ensures our future, the one I wish to talk to you about today: the route of rebuilding a sovereign, united and democratic Europe … I would today like to say with resolute conviction: the Europe of today is too weak, too slow, too inefficient, but Europe alone can enable us to take action in the world, in the face of the big contemporary challenges.

It may have been only five years ago. But it was a very different age: the leading security threat to much of the world seemed to be terror; the new fashionable threat was cyber security; the European idea was being belted relentlessly by the divorce process with the British on Brexit; and Donald Trump was in the White House and raging about the hopelessness of Europe and of NATO.

Notably, even with Macron's sense of alarm about Europe's vulnerabilities, France's strategic review – and his speech – only mentioned Russia once or twice in the context of nuclear argy-bargy in the Baltics. And when I spoke to people in Germany about Russia in 2017, there was a complacency bordering on the benign about what Vladimir Putin's plans might be, despite his documented attempts to interfere in elections across Europe; the indifference was, and remains, baffling to an outsider.

Scholz models his political modus operandi on Merkel's caution

Also looming then, as now, was the prospect of the big gas pipeline from Russia – Nord Stream 2 – which offered Germany energy security and the (naive) belief that such a mutually beneficial economic arrangement would tie Russia closer to Europe, and therefore make it less of a threat, if indeed it was one at all.

Even after the annexation of Crimea three years earlier, the idea of a conventional war of the sort we have seen in 2022 in Ukraine – which looks for all the world like the traditional warfare of seventy years ago – did not seem to be on the radar. Despite these signs of German complacency, Macron – determined to rouse a Europe that was "too weak, too slow, too inefficient" – was not to be deterred. And from 2017 onwards, the process of breathing life into the idea of the EU not just being an economic union but a security union was being stubbornly progressed.

Macron began a relentless – and not necessarily very successful – attempt to drag Angela Merkel along for the ride. Gudrun Wacker observed that Merkel's foreign policy failed to adjust to the changing global environment. "It was just, 'we want to preserve what we have' … And so Macron's initiative on the EU and other initiatives, we just didn't respond."

While the ever-cautious Merkel hesitated, Macron's push dominated discussions within Europe and NATO. But then other factors intervened: in 2020, COVID interrupted much of the public focus on European security; Trump's loss of the US presidency changed the NATO dynamics; and Merkel, too, who had so dominated the European stage, departed in 2021.

At the subsequent 2021 elections in Germany, the traditional party of the left, the SPD, which had been almost obliterated in 2017, became the centre of a new and unlikely alliance government with the Greens and the free market–based Liberals, supplanting Merkel's conservative Christian Democratic Union (CDU).

The new chancellor, Olaf Scholz, was largely unknown outside Germany, and only really known as a finance minister within it.

A former mayor of Hamburg, Scholz models his political modus operandi on Merkel's caution – always the last person in the room to talk. Like much of the SPD, he was seen as being unreliable, or at least less likely to be assertive, when it came to dealing with Russia, because of old socialist ties. These perceptions of the SPD had been coloured by an ongoing controversy surrounding the close ties of former SPD chancellor Gerhard Schröder to Russian business interests.

There was also scepticism about the capacity of the Greens foreign minister, Annalena Baerbock (though she proved to take a harder line against Putin than Scholz). These perceptions of the new government set the tone for much that happened in its first few months, during the ominous build-up of rhetoric and materiel around Ukraine's borders.

Looking back, the analysis in Europe – and around the world – was striking on a number of fronts and is worth recalling to show how much has changed.

Most notably, the overwhelming presumption in the West was that Putin would not mount a full-scale invasion ("that would be mad!"), despite all the intelligence that showed him massing troops on the borders. Second was the presumption that, if Putin invaded, Ukraine would succumb within days. And then the debate would be about where he would head next. Beyond the military issues, there were also presumptions that Germany would not act against Russia: in particular, that it would never cancel the Nord Stream 2 deal, nor that it would fundamentally change its resistance to greater military spending.

These assessments came amid a deliberate strategy, led by the US, of announcing what exactly the Russians were doing and planning. But all that intelligence missed that the Russian military was in a state of haphazard disorganisation and that Ukraine had sizable stockpiles of military resources, and resilience.

That is, it seemed countries which would now regard themselves as Ukraine's allies knew more about the enemy than their friends. It is possible that the West's presumptions proved so wrong because, in the period surrounding the invasion and the months immediately afterwards, the bulk of materiel that moved in to assist Ukraine came from the Eastern members of NATO. Notably Poland.

There was eminent sense in this: Poland and other Eastern European countries still had large quantities of Russian, even Soviet-era, hardware. The Ukrainians were familiar with how to use it, unlike gear from the US, Germany or other countries, for which they would need training. As the flow of direct military aid to Ukraine subsequently grew, there was also a significant shifting of more modern arms to these Eastern states to replenish what had been sent south. Not only had the war in Ukraine achieved the exact opposite of what Vladimir Putin wanted – by hardening the resolve and expanding the members of NATO – it helped produce a significant modernisation and improved capability of many of the NATO members that bristled at Russia's borders.

"Yes. President Macron had described NATO as brain dead," says David McAllister, a German member of the European Parliament and chair of its foreign affairs committee. "Yes, President Trump was talking about NATO being obsolete. Well, quite the contrary, NATO is back, as the English would say. NATO is alive and kicking."

But there was still the question of what the Germans would do.

In February, we got an answer.

Five days before the Russian invasion of Ukraine began, Chancellor Scholz had told the Munich Security Conference on 19 February, "We need aeroplanes that fly, ships that can set out to sea and soldiers who are optimally equipped for their missions."

Three days later, he surprised most observers by suspending the Nord Stream 2 project.

And then, on 27 February, he gave a speech in the Bundestag that has become known as the *Zeitenwende* (or turning point) speech. "Putin's war marks a turning point – and that goes for our foreign policy, too," Scholz said. He continued:

> The issue at the heart of this is whether power is allowed to prevail over the law. Whether we permit Putin to turn back the clock to the nineteenth century and the age of the great powers. Or whether we have it in us to keep warmongers like Putin in check. That requires strength of our own.

The crucial part of the speech was in the specific commitments he made about military spending. The Bundeswehr, he said, needed new capabilities and the nation had to "invest much more in the security of our country", a "major national undertaking". He announced a new special fund for the Bundeswehr which would receive an initial one-off allocation of 100 billion euros, and committed to annual defence spending of at least 2 per cent of GDP. "The goal is a powerful, cutting-edge, progressive Bundeswehr that can be relied upon to protect us."

It is hard to overstate the significance of this shift on military spending across Europe: Germany was not just throwing off the language and strategies of the past, but its actions were compelling other NATO members to increase their spending too. Many smaller countries had been happy to hide behind Germany's failure to meet the commitment to 2 per cent military spending to avoid increasing their own.

The speech also reflected the perhaps unexpected internal dynamics of the new German government. While the conservative CDU had prevaricated for years, a combination of socialists, Greens and free marketeers were now taking a harder line against Russia and a more aggressive defence position.

David McAllister said:

> Looking back there will be a European history of a twenty-first century before and after the 24th of February ... The remarkable thing is that the German CDU/CSU [the CDU's Bavarian sister party] was always in favour of more defence expenditure. And it was our socialist coalition partner who was always blocking this.

I mean, sometimes history writes strange stories: Olaf Scholz was the exact same finance minister who blocked this. And now he's calling for increasing the expenditure.

McAllister's remarks reflect a bipartisan support for the *Zeitenwende* but also a scepticism about – and possible explanation for – why nothing significant has happened since the speech.

The dramatic change in rhetoric has not been matched by any material outline of how it will affect Germany's strategic positioning, or even its role within Europe. "Olaf Scholz's problems are in his own party. The left wing of the German socialists is traditionally very pacifist, very sceptical towards the German armed forces," McAllister says.

Ben Schreer, executive director of the International Institute for Strategic Studies, agrees it was "a great speech but I think it came about in the context of enormous pressure on the chancellor to do something because domestic opinion was turning".

Foreign governments were putting huge pressure on Germany; the SPD was on the defensive. The speech immediately raised a lot of expectations ... only then to [see Scholz] walk back [from his apparent commitments] in the following weeks. The government continues to send rather mixed signals on what kind of weapons it will send to Ukraine.

Roderich Kiesewetter, who is the special representative of the CDU/CSU in the Bundestag's Foreign Affairs Committee, says something similar, observing that the *Zeitenwende* "was a double [turning point]", not just at the national level but also "inside the SPD, also in parts of the Greens".

But, he says, there remains scepticism about how seriously the SPD is really prepared to change tack with Russia. "The applause was so great and big that it was also kind of a push forward for the chancellor. But he didn't make use of it. Until the end of April, we delivered a lot of small weapons, and some anti-tank and anti-aircraft weapons. But since the end of April until today, until this week, except for the howitzers, nothing was delivered, nothing substantial."

The *Zeitenwende* was not just about the shift in Germany's defence and foreign policy but also its economic relationships – which have forced it to do an inelegant volte-face on energy policy and climate change. Having led the surge towards renewables and closed down its nuclear energy capacity, Germany has raced to build gas storage and revitalise coal-fired power plants following the sudden spectre of the loss of gas supplies from Russia. But even with these huge changes in strategic positioning and energy policy, Ben Schreer says, one crucial question "wasn't resolved".

"And that is this question of leadership, of German leadership. In Europe, the Germans find it very difficult to formulate a leadership ambition, despite the fact that it is the biggest power in continental

Europe," he notes. Scholz's speech may have raised expectations, particularly in smaller countries that Germany would now lead, he says, "because who else is there to lead?"

"Instead, Scholz has been extraordinarily persistent in his message that Germany will only act in line with what our allies want, which, to me sometimes sounds like, 'we will do what the Americans want us to do', even if it takes a while."

Schreer observes that it has been primarily the Americans who provided support to Ukraine through training and intelligence, and by spending more than the entire EU. "Without the Americans, I think the Ukraine support would have been seriously in jeopardy."

But many in Europe are painfully aware that the United States, though it may have led in the past, has its own problems now – none more so than its strategic competition with China. Macron of course remains keen to lead, but his proposals for greater political integration – let alone a common defence policy – have made little headway with his fellow Europeans.

Political integration – at a time when the EU has been so preoccupied with Brexit, and with tensions with new members in the East – is probably just a little too ambitious. While many European countries might understand the benefits of a common defence policy, few want to give up their defence industry autonomy, and often view the Macron proposals with the suspicion of business competitors.

The debate about what has happened to Germany's ambitions since the *Zeitenwende* speech is not just a rhetorical one. There has been considerable confusion about exactly what the spending commitments entailed and whether it was enough to bring the military's materiel up to scratch. Most analysts say the 100 billion euros mentioned by Scholz in February, if spread over, say, three years, would barely touch the sides.

Ben Schreer says he is "not sure that the majority of particularly the SPD is really comfortable with a new approach towards Russia".

> This government really still struggles to say, "We really have to help Ukraine win the war. We really have to put the security interests of middle and Eastern European and Baltic countries into the centre, as opposed to [ensuring] some kind of relationship with Russia after all of this is over." Baerbock is much more comfortable in saying, "They are fighting our war and we need to make Russia lose this war, whatever we're losing."

Schreer is one of the few people I speak to in Germany who speaks of Russia losing the war. This is not because people assume Russia will eventually win. It's more complicated than that. Yes, there is an element of finding it hard to get beyond the mythical concept of the Russian military as a creature of infinite and inexhaustible resources, even given all the blunders and massive losses of men and materiel so spectacularly on display in the early months of the war.

It is that analysts do not believe Putin will allow Russia to be defeated. That is, if he thinks he is going to lose, he will turn to the nuclear option. On many levels, Putin's actions can be seen as a strategic failure. If his goal was to stop the expansion of the membership of NATO and the EU, he has achieved the exact opposite. But from a European perspective, that only makes things more dangerous. By escalating the ongoing skirmishing – Putin calls it a "special military operation" – to the formal definition of a war, it has also escalated the stakes.

The result is that it is often difficult to get those in the strategic community in Germany to define what a Ukrainian "victory" would look like: would it be a settlement of borders that recognise some of Russia's gains, or something much harder line?

Europe and Australia are likely to need each other more amid the growing power of authoritarian regimes

Even with all the uncertainty about Germany and its leadership within Europe, the *Zeitenwende* has given new impetus to the idea of a European defence strategy.

The discussion now revolves around what, in the best EU traditions, is known as the Strategic Compass, adopted at the end of March, and which sits alongside a new NATO Strategic Concept. The Compass is very much a product of all the pushing by France and particularly Macron, who is now heading the revolving presidency of the European Union.

In 2017, after Macron first won office, he announced an ambitious proposal to establish a "common intervention force, a common defence budget and a common doctrine for action", including an acceleration of the Permanent Structured Cooperation (PESCO) – a plan to integrate national European armed forces. That means bringing together everything from the intelligence gathering of armed forces to defence industries. The long-discussed "European tank" to replace the plethora of different tanks built across Europe is a prime example.

The Strategic Compass is of a piece with the PESCO idea, but when it was announced this year, the plans were still modest: an EU Rapid Deployment Capacity of up to 5000 personnel; live exercises on land and at sea; and plans for more rapid and flexible decision-making.

Macron also pushed his European partners to establish an EU defence fund, which is supposed to support European technology and industry research and development.

So there are now these two sets of alliances, or common projects, sitting side by side. There is the NATO military alliance, which promises security and defence for all members. Then there is the idea of the EU, spreading its wings from an economic cooperation project, to a community with a common system of law making, and now, its proponents hope, a cooperative union of agreed defence goals in areas where a traditional alliance like NATO doesn't go. For example, there is the simple but important question of military mobility (things like being able to get materiel from one side of Europe to the other in a hurry and crossing into countries that may not be members of NATO).

David McAllister says:

> We in Europe have to become quicker. If you want to transport a US tank, let's say from Rotterdam to Riga, you have to go through many, many European countries. That involves a lot of paperwork. We have to reduce paperwork, but we also have to modernise our infrastructure … so that you can actually transport heavy military equipment from the west of Europe – from the Atlantic ports – to the eastern flank, or from the north seaports to the southern flank.

Europe has to become quicker. Germany has to become quicker.

We tend to view the old world of Europe as having a different set of problems to the ones we face, because of the heavy layers of history which shape it. But Germany now faces a very similar problem to Australia. Instead of quickening our defensive responses to a challenging regional environment, we seem to have slowed them down through decisions like AUKUS – and the delays entail not just actual military hardware but the repositioning of our strategic thinking.

Europe and Australia are likely to need each other more amid the growing power of authoritarian regimes. We would do well to better recognise and understand Europe's strengths and vulnerabilities – and the forces that underlie them. ■

LESSON FOR TAIWAN

Invasion is hard

Gwynne Dyer

Taiwan should draw two lessons from the war in Ukraine. One is that the United States will not fight China to protect Taiwan from an invasion any more than it has gone to war with Russia to save Ukraine. However, the same reasoning suggests that the United States would probably do everything short of war with China to help Taiwan – provided that Taiwan could put up a good show of resistance in the first days of an attempted Chinese invasion.

The other lesson is that Taiwan could still make a Chinese invasion very difficult if, like Ukraine, it prioritises defence above all else and makes realistic preparations. The odds against Taiwan are longer than they were for Ukraine in terms of population (70–1 for China versus Taiwan compared to 3–1 for Russia versus Ukraine). They are also pretty long against Taiwan in terms of GDP: around 22–1 in China's favour. But Taiwan (unlike Ukraine) is an island surrounded by an ocean, and that evens things up quite a bit.

The June launch of China's first full-service aircraft carrier in Shanghai marked another big step in the country's steady advance towards what the US armed forces call "peer rival" status. The country's first two carriers were a small Russian cast-off and a cheap Chinese knock-off version of that, but the *Fujian* is an 80,000-tonne behemoth equipped with electromagnetic catapults and all the other mod cons.

It will take the Chinese navy another three to five years to hone the skills needed to sustain a fast pace of combat operations on a fleet carrier, and much longer to move up to the three or four full-size carriers that it would need to challenge the US Pacific Fleet's command of the broader Western Pacific. In terms of military aircraft and non-strategic missiles, however, for all practical purposes China is already technologically a peer competitor to the United States.

China's aircraft-launched "carrier-killer" hypersonic missiles would severely restrict US carrier operations within 1000 kilometres of the Chinese coast in wartime. Only one base is available to US land-based air power within unrefuelled range of Taiwan (Kadena Air Base on Okinawa), compared to forty Chinese air bases within range. It will not appear in any published official documents, but it is very likely that the US Navy has already concluded that directly participating in the defence of Taiwan would be unwise in any Chinese invasion scenario in which the US has not already disabled east coast Chinese air and missile facilities. And to take out those facilities, of course, would mean war with China.

We may, therefore, conclude that the United States, regardless of what it says in public, will not go to war to defend Taiwan. Even disregarding the risk of an escalation to nuclear weapons, the potential cost of fighting a naval and air war with China off its own coast and 11,000 kilometres from the United States has become far too high, given that the security or even the existence of a separate government in Taiwan is not a vital American national interest. President Joe Biden's new habit of uttering apparently off-the-cuff promises to do exactly that (only to have those commitments walked back by his staff) may be an attempt to restore China's fading belief that he would be willing to do such an implausible thing.

The traditional "strategic ambiguity" about whether the United States would actually fight to defend Taiwan is gone. It definitely won't. China already knew that even before it saw the American response to Russia's invasion of Ukraine. Indeed, Beijing's bold new claim that the Taiwan Strait is not international waters, made repeatedly to American officials in recent months, suggests that Beijing is already thinking of the day when it can deny free passage through those waters to warships of other nations.

This does not mean that Xi Jinping's regime has decided to invade Taiwan soon, or indeed ever. The official Chinese position, reiterated in June by Minister of National Defense Wei Fenghe at the IISS Shangri-La Dialogue in Singapore, remains: "If anyone dares to secede Taiwan from China, we will not hesitate to fight. We will fight at all costs. And we will fight to the very end. This is the only choice for China." Since Taipei would never formally secede – indeed, its historical claim to represent the only legitimate government of all China makes such a declaration constitutionally impossible – Beijing's official policy poses no threat to the island's de facto independence. The reality, of course, is somewhat different.

Beijing emits enough fire-breathing rhetoric about "reuniting the motherland by force" to justify concern in Taipei about a cross-strait invasion – although not enough, as yet, to motivate Taipei to undertake a renovation and reinforcement of its run-down and understaffed armed forces. On the other hand, the multiple failures of the Russian armed forces in attempting a much simpler military operation in Ukraine will undoubtedly be giving senior Chinese commanders cause to rethink their views on the prospects for carrying out a quick seaborne invasion of Taiwan. And President Xi will doubtless be contemplating the parlous position of Russia's President Vladimir Putin and his stalled invasion of Ukraine.

"Collective leadership" is dead in Russia and dying in China. Trying to read the minds of increasingly isolated one-man regimes is a futile activity, so without delving further into the likelihood of a cross-strait Chinese attack on Taiwan, this article will consider whether Taiwan's current defence policy and preparations could deter or defeat such a Chinese invasion attempt without direct American military intervention and, if not, whether such a policy is even possible.

There has been no public acknowledgement by Taipei that the country's implicit dependence on American military support to deter an invasion no longer works. That makes perfectly good sense. There is no benefit for Taiwan in openly recognising that reality so long as it retains even a shred of credibility – unless the government decides to build the capacity to defend the island on its own. That would be extremely expensive, and the government would then need to convince the public that such expenditure was necessary and likely to be effective.

However, neither Taiwan's military commanders nor President Tsai Ing-wen's government are fantasists. They will be well aware that the People's Republic's rising military power has reached a tipping point, after which dependence on that ambiguous American guarantee is no longer an adequate strategy. They will be urgently considering their remaining political and military options, and finding them quite limited.

The recent destruction of Hong Kong's civil liberties by the PRC effectively extinguishes the plausibility of a comparable "one country, two systems" arrangement that preserves Taiwan's civil liberties while accepting Beijing's sovereignty over the island. The remaining available options are the status quo or surrender, and the status quo will only survive if Taiwan can come up with a defence policy that works without active US military support.

In principle, such a policy would require Taipei to possess nuclear weapons, since the PRC could otherwise use its own nukes to force Taiwan into surrender. It's all but certain that Taiwan has not secretly developed or acquired such weapons in the past, and there's zero chance that it could do so now. However, there is also a strong belief on both sides of the Taiwan Strait that no leadership in Beijing would choose the perpetual infamy of using nuclear weapons on fellow Chinese, so we need only examine the possibility that Taiwan could successfully resist a non-nuclear Chinese invasion attempt on its own for some significant period of time.

It could not do so now, for it has long assumed (or at least chosen to hope) that the American policy of strategic ambiguity was simply a device to minimise friction with China, and that the US Navy and Air Force, if not American ground troops, would show up when they were needed. That was never really certain, and is now palpably untrue. However, Taiwan probably could resist a Chinese invasion attempt on its own if it took the necessary measures in advance. Being an island in the ocean has certain advantages.

If "reunification" is Beijing's Holy Grail, then smashing Taiwan up is not enough

It is certainly possible for Beijing to "bomb [Taiwan] back into the Stone Age", to borrow US Air Force general Curtis Lemay's colourful phrase. (He was talking about North Vietnam.) The entire island, including its east coast, is within 250 kilometres of China, which is only a few minutes' flight time for short-range ballistic missiles.

China already has 450 short-range ballistic missiles based along the coast facing Taiwan and is adding at least seventy-five a year. If it decided to simply batter Taiwan into the ground, it could easily expand that number into the thousands – enough to crater every runway, collapse every road and train bridge, and destroy every harbour, dam and power plant on the island.

Taiwan is considering the purchase of state-of-the-art anti-missile weapons in response (it currently has only some first-generation Patriot missile batteries), but China's vastly greater resources would allow it to saturate and overwhelm any imaginable expansion of Taiwanese anti-missile defences. Taiwan has also built its own short-range ballistic missiles, including one, the Yun Feng missile, that can just about reach Beijing with a favourable tailwind, but once again China can out-produce it 10–1. The bitter truth is that Taiwan cannot win a missile exchange; it can be beaten into the ground from afar.

However, if "reunification" is Beijing's Holy Grail, then smashing Taiwan up is not enough. "Unification" necessarily involves taking control of the entire island of Taiwan, destroying its government, expunging the symbols of its separate existence and imposing rule from Beijing. Imagine, if you will, a Taiwan whose military and civil infrastructure has been virtually levelled but whose government and people are still snarling defiance at the mainland regime. Would that be an acceptable outcome for the government of Xi Jinping or any like-minded successor? Obviously not. An actual invasion has to be the final act in any Chinese attack on Taiwan – and that is where things get tricky for Beijing.

River crossings are hard, as any experienced soldier knows. River crossings with the enemy on the far side are ten times harder, and can be very costly in lives and time. And landings from the sea on a defended coast are just about the most difficult operation an army can undertake. Although the Taiwan Strait is only 130 to 180 kilometres wide, it really is an ocean crossing, which makes the task even harder.

A little military history here. There is almost no pre-twentieth-century history of assault landings on defended coasts, because until that time fleets of ships could move much faster along a coastline than armies could march overland. Just sail to a part of the coast that the defending army hasn't reached yet and ferry your soldiers, cannon and supplies ashore in boats. By the time the defenders arrive, everybody will be safely on land and ready to fight.

Railways changed everything: for the first time in history travel was quicker by land than by sea. This began to be a problem for generals trying to get armies ashore on a hostile coast as early as the American Civil War of the 1860s, but few railways then ran along the coasts, road transport was still horse-and-cart, and the Union navy enjoyed absolute superiority at sea, so Union troops could land pretty much anywhere they wanted. By World War I it was very different.

The British, French and Anzac landings at Gallipoli on the Turkish Straits in 1915 – intended to knock the Ottoman Empire out of the war and open the way for Russia to export its grain and for its allies to send it supplies – were a catastrophic failure. Turkish soldiers were waiting for them in positions overlooking the landing beaches, and machine guns and artillery decimated the soldiers struggling through the surf and seeking shelter on bare beaches. The Allies tried further landings over a period of eight months, but never got more than a few kilometres inland. In Australian national mythology it was all because the British generals were stupid, and the British blamed it all on Winston Churchill (then First Lord of the Admiralty), but it was a revelation to everybody.

The modern doctrine of amphibious warfare, which made assault landings against defended beaches almost commonplace during World War II, was developed by the United States Marine Corps between the two world wars and codified for the first time in the *Tentative Landing Operations Manual* of 1935, which even described the specialised landing craft that would be needed. Everybody knows about the rules and the right equipment by now, but it is still the most difficult large-scale military operation to carry out successfully. Since Taiwan's west coast, facing China, is only about 400 kilometres long – even counting all the inlets and headlands – any Chinese landing on Taiwan would have to be an assault landing against well-prepared defenders – or, rather, Taiwan could make that a reality if it chooses to.

Taiwan's defence spending has been rather modest in the past several decades, with any idea of reconquering the mainland long forgotten and high confidence that the US would intervene to stop a Chinese attack. There was always an element of wishful thinking in this, but Taipei did not rethink its strategy even as the rhetoric in Beijing grew harsher and the balance of forces in the Western Pacific shifted gradually in China's favour. Taiwan's 2022 defence budget was still only US$17 billion for a country of 24 million people. That's 2.1 per cent of Taiwan's GDP, which is almost exactly the same share of GDP that Australia devotes to defence. One would have thought that by last year Taiwan was feeling a lot more vulnerable than Australia, but apparently not so.

That is beginning to change, as Taiwan's government wakes up to the reality of American foreign policy: in January, the parliament in Taipei voted an extra US$8.6 billion for defence (spread over the next five years). But it may end up being a great deal more than that. Tsai's government is only beginning to come to terms with the fact that Taiwan is going to be almost completely responsible for its own defence in the event of an attempted Chinese invasion, at least in the early phases. If it survives those, it might begin to receive arms and financial help from a few friendly governments (particularly the United States and Japan), but even then it would have to depend exclusively on its own troops.

Post-Mao governments in Beijing … essentially put the Taiwan question on the backburner

That is a very tall order, but not necessarily an impossible one if (a) China does not use or threaten to use nuclear weapons; (b) Taiwan develops an intelligent and well-funded defence strategy; and (c) it is very lucky.

Let's be frank: the survival of the "Republic of China" for almost three-quarters of a century after the Kuomintang (Nationalists; KMT) lost the Chinese Civil War in 1949 and withdrew to Taiwan was a historical accident. It was only possible because the new regime on the mainland, led by Mao Zedong (or Mao Tse-tung, as it was written in English during his lifetime), failed to develop China economically for three decades (1950–1980).

Most of East Asia's early industry had been destroyed in the wars of the 1930s and '40s, so once peace was restored (1945 for Japan, 1949 for China, 1953 for Korea) a period of rapid economic growth was hardly surprising. However, the People's Republic of China somehow missed the bus.

In 1950, per capita GDP in all three East Asian countries was under US$100 a year. In 1985, it was US$10,000 in Japan and US$7000 in South Korea, as cheap labour flooded into the cities to work in the new factories, prompting a sustained three-decade burst of 10 per cent per annum economic growth. Yet, in the Chinese People's Republic, GDP per capita in 1985 was still only US$300 a year.

There was no profound structural or cultural reason why China should lag behind, and indeed Chinese people in Taiwan turned in a respectable performance despite a large burden of refugees and huge defence expenditures: Taiwan had a GDP per capita of US$3300 by 1985. You can't even blame the failure on communism: the old Soviet Union had a comparable period of high-speed growth between the end of the Civil War in 1920 and the German invasion in 1941, and the second generation of Chinese communist leaders, from Deng Xiaoping to Hu Jintao, belatedly delivered the statutory East Asian three decades of 10 per cent growth for their country from 1985 to 2015. (Economic growth is now falling back to a normal developed-country rate under Xi Jinping.)

It was Mao Zedong who single-handedly prevented the Chinese economy from taking off for a quarter-century with his ceaseless, furious political campaigns, from the “Great Leap Forward” (1958–62) to the “Cultural Revolution” (1966–76). Tens of millions died needlessly, and the country stayed very poor. Mao’s regime was extremely hostile to the Kuomintang in Taiwan throughout his rule, but he lacked the means to do anything about it.

Post-Mao governments in Beijing, starting with Deng Xiaoping’s, prioritised economic growth and essentially put the Taiwan question on the backburner. They also developed a huge and economically vital trade with the United States and other Western economies, which militated against an attempt to seize Taiwan that might damage those trading relationships. This afforded Taiwan time to transform itself into a prosperous and democratic society.

The Kuomintang’s brutal one-party rule gradually softened after the death of Chiang Kai-shek in 1975, the establishment of the first opposition party in 1986, and the democratic election of 2000, in which the KMT finally lost power. While Beijing continued to insist throughout this period that Taiwan was a Chinese province illegally alienated from central rule, and conducted a persistent and largely successful campaign to persuade other nations to switch their diplomatic relations from Taipei to Beijing, there was little urgency in its ritual condemnations of Taiwan’s de facto separate status. It’s no wonder that successive democratically elected governments in Taipei gave defence spending a relatively low priority.

That period is now at an end.

If Taiwan is now truly on its own, at least until it has demonstrated the will and ability to blunt a Chinese invasion attempt, what are the requirements that would deliver that capability?

It must be able to withstand a long-range bombardment by thousands of Chinese short-range ballistic missiles – presumably accompanied by cruise missile attacks and manned air strikes – that target virtually all above-ground military facilities and likely many elements of the country's infrastructure as well. Whether or not the civilian population would be directly attacked is impossible to predict, but strategically almost irrelevant.

It must retain the ability, under this kind of bombardment, to attack and sink at least a large proportion of the ships bringing Chinese ground troops across the Taiwan Strait, and similarly to intercept and bring down the majority of the aircraft that attempt to drop airborne troops onto the island.

It must build and maintain an army that is able to fight under these circumstances and confine invading Chinese troops who do manage to establish lodgements on Taiwanese soil to their beachheads and drop zones, eventually "mopping them up".

And it should probably be able to go on doing this for at least several weeks without striking back directly at the Chinese airfields, missile sites and harbours from which the attack is coming. As with Ukraine's defensive war with Russia, making it clear to the world that Taiwan is waging a purely defensive struggle against China would be more important than doing a bit of damage to Chinese military facilities on the mainland. (A little sabotage would be permissible.)

If the Taiwanese were successful in hanging on for a couple of weeks, Washington and Tokyo might then decide that they were morally obliged to resupply Taiwan with weapons and use their navies to prevent a permanent Chinese blockade of the island. Or they might not. It would depend on the geopolitical situation in the world at the moment when these events occur.

"We will become a 'big Israel' ... I am confident that the question of security will be the [number-one issue]"

The goal of such a strategy would not be military victory for Taiwan. That is not an available option. It would be, first of all, to create a credible deterrent by making it clear that the military cost of a Chinese invasion would be very high and the outcome uncertain. If deterrence failed, the goal would be to create a military stalemate, where Chinese forces have suffered heavy losses but failed to create any lasting presence on Taiwan, and ideally where "Western" powers (including Japan) have been goaded and shamed into offering the island state at least some limited support.

The cost of this strategy would be very high: at least a long-term doubling of Taiwan's military spending, but more probably a tripling – say, 6 per cent of GDP. It would also entail a substantial militarisation of Taiwanese society.

It's a strategy that would require several million trained soldiers, so that any Chinese military footholds in Taiwan could be rapidly eliminated. Compulsory military service, reduced to four months in 2017, is already coming under review. Less than a month after Russia's invasion of Ukraine, Minister of National Defense Chiu Kuo-cheng told parliament that putting the term of conscription back up to one year is being actively considered, though the decision would not be "announced today and implemented tomorrow". It could end up being even longer than that, with an obligation for a cadre of reservists several million strong to stay current in military matters after their national service by annual refreshers on the model of the Israeli or Swiss reserves.

In this context, Taiwanese citizens should consider what President Volodymyr Zelenskyy said in April about Ukraine's future next to a much bigger enemy that is obsessed with destroying it, with little hope of joining an alliance that would oblige its friends to protect it:

> Ukraine will definitely not be what we wanted it to be from the beginning. It is impossible. Absolutely liberal, European – it will not be like that. We will become a "big Israel" ... I am confident that the question of security will be the issue number one for the next ten years. I am sure of it.

Ukrainians will accept that fate because they have already been invaded, and they understand that the cost of being conquered is cultural extinction. Taiwan has not been invaded and may never be (although the likelihood is higher than it used to be). So, the question becomes: would today's prosperous and well-educated Taiwanese society, with a lifestyle and an outlook not all that different from that of its counterparts in Japan or America, really be willing to accept such a level of sacrifice, for so long, for such an uncertain outcome? For there is really no guarantee that even these extreme measures could save it from invasion and subjugation.

What is so unique about Taiwan's culture that it must be preserved at any cost? Its indigenous traditions, certainly: the island is the homeland of the Austronesian culture, whose people migrated south to populate most of the islands of the Indian and Pacific Oceans, from Madagascar to Easter Island. The Chinese settlers who arrived in Taiwan in large numbers from the 1760s, only a couple of decades before British settlers arrived in Australia, mistreated and despised the indigenous peoples in the usual settler way for a long time. They account for only 2 per cent of the population today, but the "First Nations" and their traditions are at last getting some respect from the majority.

As for the settlers, however, they really haven't been there long enough to develop a unique culture. Taiwan was largely neglected by the Qing dynasty, fell under Japanese rule in 1895, and since then has only been governed from Beijing for four years (1945–49). Chinese-speaking Taiwanese are no more different from mainland Chinese than New Zealanders are from Australians, but their political experience has been very different. Political freedom is their main reason for wanting to remain separate, and only they can decide whether preserving a democratic society is important enough to them to justify the sacrifice and the risk that maintaining that status requires.

Of course, they may simply decide to dodge the question. Indeed, that may be the likeliest outcome. A defence policy that responds realistically to Taiwan's changed strategic circumstances – no more American "guarantee" – would involve so much expense and such upheaval in people's lives that they may prefer to stick with the current arrangements and take their chances on the future. After all, Xi Jinping is mortal, and China has been banging on about "unification" for decades without ever doing anything about it. It may never happen, many Taiwanese tell themselves – and who's to say they are wrong?

Annexing Taiwan would add little more to the strength of the Chinese state or the wealth of its people than capturing the Falkland Islands would do for Argentina. The scandalous "division" of China is a useful grievance for the Chinese regime to exploit when it needs to stimulate nationalist fervour and distract public opinion from some other problem, but conquering Taiwan would end its usefulness. Besides, China may be heading for economic stagnation, demographic decline and/or a climate disaster. As the great American baseballer Yogi Berra pointed out, "Predictions are hard, especially about the future."

And there is such a thing as buying too much insurance. ■

PENNY WONG

Testing herself and Australia

Geraldine Doogue

"To whom much is given, much will be required," to quote Luke 12:48. So what will be asked of the prodigiously talented Penny Wong, Australia's new foreign minister, who was on public display at Japan's Quad meeting just twenty-four hours after the election?

In many eyes, she is the ultimate proof Australia has "arrived" as a country moving fast beyond its Anglo-Saxon-Celt roots. If only Lee Kuan Yew were alive to see it. Even he might have suspended his usual scepticism about Australia's commitment to belonging in its neighbourhood.

Yes, the sight of an Australian foreign minister, of mixed heritage, confidently messaging in Bahasa Indonesian and Malay during her first official South-East Asian visit in June was stunning – prompting delight within Australia and bemused astonishment in the Asian region. How much the imagery influences genuine Asian rethinking of our attitudes is still to be settled. But the "optics" were a circuit-breaker from the past. Even among the usual critics, images like these prompted exuberant pride in the nation's multicultural achievements. But it also brought big expectations that Wong herself may not exactly welcome.

Late last year, while obviously considering the possibility of government, she told an ANU National Security Conference in Canberra that our region was being reshaped, and that this generation of political leaders bore a big responsibility in the reshaping. "We are in a contest – a race, you might say, for influence." The question is, where will she (on our behalf) put most of her energies to follow through on this correct assessment? Where will she be tested? Where will she need to take risks? "Surely it's obvious," a friend offered instantly in answer to my questions, "it depends on how she handles China."

I have come to believe something different. That her big test is less obvious yet will matter equally to our country's future: how she'll manage the Americans, our great and powerful friend, though a declining power, wrestling with the burden of maintaining its dominance in Asia. And this brings specific challenges for Australia, if you accept the argument advanced by the veteran analyst Hugh White, among others. And I do now, having reflected over time on what might lie ahead.

It has been striking, researching this piece, to see the column inches devoted to how Australia, via Wong and her boss, Anthony Albanese, will deal with Chinese demands. That is self-evidently a true challenge. Yet there is much less curiosity about how Australia might convey to the US any serious shifts in our capacity to trust its ongoing commitment.

Doubtless this is appropriate risk analysis. Are we not all constantly scanning the uncertainties within our region and beyond, heightened by the drama in Ukraine? Those uncertainties extend to the health of the American republic itself.

While the Americans, in my experience, are most definitely capable of self-criticism, they do not generally welcome it from others, certainly not from "reliable" Australia. And if White and others are right, it won't be criticism anyway, but rather warnings about the risks that lie ahead for them and us in this dynamic region, where one super-fast-growing power, China, wants to establish primacy over its particular zone of the world, namely East Asia and the Western Pacific. That doesn't necessarily mean a prelude to war, rather the achievement of super-power status akin to that of the US and the Soviets during the Cold War. And if we're lucky, China might then settle for the idea of participating in a multilateral framework that keeps the peace.

How do we Australians truly consider our place in Asia

If we're not lucky, the prospects for war in our region, with all its attendant horrors, rise exponentially. Australian corporate memory is rightly haunted by the lessons of 1942, when the much-trusted British Empire failed to protect us from an expanding Asian power, namely Japan. The acute shock we experienced, facilitating our turn to the US, should never be forgotten. A new era presents its own dilemmas, with unique tests for diplomats, politicians and military planners. But the searing realisation that great powers can be vulnerable is surely to be respected.

America is still pre-eminent in a range of ways – economically, militarily, technologically, ideologically – as White acknowledged, speaking to a gathering at a Melbourne bookshop in July. But it's just not the unchallenged global power anymore, which it doesn't seem to accept. "I think we are underestimating China and overestimating the US – an old mistake," he said. "I have never said we should walk away from the US alliance. Just be more realistic. We need to have a good chat with America about its future in Asia. That they can't expect our support unless they have some clearly achievable objectives; that they need to recast their diplomacy in Asia and they need to be talking to China."

Professor Michael Wesley, deputy vice-chancellor international at the University of Melbourne, hopes above all that the Asia-Pacific's moves towards a multipolar order preoccupy Wong. "This will require much more sophistication and nuance in Australia's statecraft," he told me. "Australia's current enthusiasm for the Quad is dividing Australia from South-East Asia, which rejects the polarising logic of the grouping. We need to find a way of shaping the Quad away from confrontational stances towards a pragmatic engagement of China, India, Japan and the US in finding a stable and open Asia Pacific."

These will be among Penny Wong's challenges: to convey respectfully, face-to-face, an ambivalence, or prudent wariness, about US abilities and "stick-ability". About what is being asked of us, as junior allies. Also to convey a confidence about our own identity within this fluid region. As Allan Gyngell concluded in Australian Foreign Affairs 15, Australian foreign policy has the chance to be more consequential in South-East Asia than anywhere else in the world, including the Pacific.

Maybe she'll also have to ingest a deep anxiety about whether we, Australians, can fully *depend* on anyone to protect us completely? To sit with that insecurity, as other forebears, like John Curtin, have done. Then not let that anxiety cripple her or her management of contemporary foreign policy. The real prize would be converting that concern into good public debate. How do we Australians truly consider our place in Asia *if* we cannot be absolutely sure the Americans will stay, expend lives and money on our safety or even win a war with China? That is a tough assignment for Wong.

Her response to these conditions is to find a "strategic equilibrium" in the Indo-Pacific, as she outlined to the International Institute of Strategic Studies in Singapore in July. But Richard Maude, a veteran diplomat who authored the last Foreign Policy White Paper in 2017, suggested this would not be easy. "It will require all arms of Australian statecraft bent to a singular, unifying objective that is agreed by the National Security Committee of Cabinet and communicated to the Australian public. It will require coordinated cooperation with partners" he wrote in *The Australian Financial Review*.

The only answer, in what amounted to a brutal struggle for power in our region, he opined, was a wide-ranging "joined-up-government" approach, more complex than anything we'd seen thus far. Again,

I wonder, does she have the grit and stamina to both initiate this and see it through … to something better?

She's clearly pondered this a lot. Observe the vital final line of her speech in Singapore:

> Australia should always act in our national interests, not through the prism of great-power competition. At times this means disagreeing with the US – as we did with former president Trump's rejection of the global rules-based order. But it also means adding real value to our relationship with the United States through our partnerships in the region. And it requires Australia, to quote Bob Hawke, to be self-reliant within the Alliance. As I have said for many years, as a US ally, the fact is we have long ago made a choice. But that is not the end of the matter.

Five years ago, addressing a Cranlana Centre for Ethical Leadership conference in Melbourne, she set out her tent with stirring rhetoric, dipping liberally into ALP heritage:

> Since being appointed … I have drawn on Labor's rich foreign policy heritage that, from Evatt to Evans and to the present, tracks the pursuit of an independent foreign policy. Independence means that we pursue our own goals for our own purposes. Our … approach is to work with the US as it is now, not as it might once have been, or as some of its naysayers claim it's going to become.

In 2018, she spoke further to a South Australian Labor conference:

> Labor will bring what we know best, working together collectively to achieve collective goods to our foreign policy. What I call constructive internationalism builds on the work that was begun by Gareth Evans twenty-five years ago. It recognises that the key to a prosperous and secure Australia is an international rules-based order where the rule-makers are also rule-takers, and where the rules are negotiated and not imposed. And it is through this approach that Labor will seek to deal with the global problems too challenging for an individual nation to address alone.

Both those speeches were delivered while preparing for a Shorten government, which of course did not eventuate. Arguably, she benefited from that enforced extra apprenticeship. Those three long years bequeathed her precious time to learn the craft of diplomacy, its language, nuances and habits.

She can't have missed either, that the department she now heads and relies upon, foreign affairs and trade (DFAT), has declined considerably in status within Canberra. A once mighty entity, this diminishment prompts acute distress among its many alumni. It is well known that the Morrison government lost confidence in the department's advice. That National Security Committee mentioned by Richard Maude is the powerbroker now, its operations keenly followed and attended, with diplomacy believed to be playing catch-up with their defence and security colleagues (or competitors?).

To achieve her ambitions for a constructive and proactive foreign policy, Wong will know she has vital work ahead restoring DFAT's reputation, let alone its budget and personnel. During her preparation in Opposition, she sharpened her inherent sense of cool demeanour under pressure. She applies well the advice frequently given to women: harness your strengths and don't dwell on any weakness you detect in yourself, let alone what others say. It's a classic rebuttal of the "imposter syndrome", where women undermine themselves by doubting their right to be there. Maybe her generation (she was born in 1968) missed this bit of self-sabotage?

According to Margaret Simons' 2019 book on Wong, *Passion and Principle*, she's regarded with a mixture of fear and respect by colleagues, who are nevertheless very loyal. I'm told she sent a rare thank-you email in her new role, acknowledging staff for their hard work serving travelling Australians during COVID. Of course, there are those flare-ups that she is known for, too, especially jousting with now OECD head Mathias Cormann in the Senate (check the entertaining YouTube clips). *Guardian Australia*'s Katharine Murphy judged them to be "choreographed not impulsive", but to the non-gallery observer, they looked pretty real. None of that will be a minus in her dealings internationally, in my view.

Certainly she brings a sort of star quality to those big decision-making tables we so earnestly seek to sit at, as Allan Gyngell puts it. Plus a sexy gravitas, effortlessly borne – surely an asset. Also maybe a small capacity to bomb-throw, remembering her early days with Young Labor in South Australia.

Her speeches and enthusiastic interaction with Solomon Islanders and Malaysians convey, too, that she has fundamentally grasped the potential winning card that is Australian multiculturalism. “The human ties of family, business, education and tourism are stronger than those of geography,” she told one Malaysian gathering. But here’s the killer paragraph: “My Malaysian heritage is one of 270 ancestries now represented in Australia. Half of Australia’s population were born overseas or have a parent who was born overseas. Australia will be reflecting this rich character back to the world so the world can see itself in Australia.” Coming from a woman born in Asia, that is a ringing endorsement without peer.

American interlocutors ... won’t take kindly to any perceived backsliding by Australia

She has learnt the formal language of the foreign affairs community, right down to standard lines such as “I want to make five key points”. It seems to be a prerequisite for being taken seriously, virtually a code that needs to be learnt in order to wrangle the ubiquitous abstractness to the ground. And to gain respect, dare I say, as a woman. This has very much been a man’s world.

James Chin, writing for the Lowy Institute *Interpreter* in July, speculated that this highly charged “soft power” represented by Wong will only work so far.

> The biggest problem is the widely held perception among the South-East Asian elites that Australia is "deputy sheriff" to the United States and will also support the US position when the chips are down. Many are sceptical that Wong (or anyone else) can change this position in the foreseeable future. Their thinking is reinforced by the AUKUS agreement and the Quad security arrangement.

Is she close, then, to developing the "galvanising narrative" towards a new strategic imagination, that Melissa Conley Tyler, an ex-diplomat now at the new Asia-Pacific Development, Diplomacy & Defence Dialogue, says is vital in setting out a big-picture vision for Australia's regional engagement?

Obviously a lot of dreaming, planning and hard labour lie ahead to bring aspirations for an independent foreign policy to fruition. What external shocks will rock any well-laid plans? Is she up for that sort of sustained debate, which won't necessarily be welcomed by some within her own party let alone others, or, for that matter, the rather narrow media? Average Australian citizens might be more available for reflection than their officials.

All this will be tested by powerful Chinese and, in my view, especially American interlocutors. They won't take kindly to any perceived backsliding by Australia. We'll be reminded of being on the right and wrong side of history, as they see it. Our dilemmas, given our history and geography, are unlikely to be treated with much sympathy.

Also, I cannot imagine that well-meaning advice giving, such as Hugh White suggests, would be appreciated. Americans flatter copiously and assume it will be returned. They turn on the charm big-time and can become rather savage if Australians seriously question their modus operandi. Without betraying Chatham House rules, I can tell you that I witnessed memorable exchanges between Americans and Australians during the Australian American Leadership Dialogues earlier this century, over issues still very much alive in public debate. Once seen, never forgotten. You're either with us or against us, is the strong sense given off by people like the former secretary of state Mike Pompeo – who could forget his aggressive demeanour during AUSMIN (Australian-United States Ministerial Consultations) 2021? – though, admittedly, not by the current occupant, Anthony Blinken, or the current defense secretary, Lloyd Austin.

I like to hope that Penny Wong is well fortified for this type of encounter. And she might console herself with the knowledge that Henry Kissinger, no less, is obsessed with leaders, statesmen (!) and prophets who "transcend crises and 'raise their society to their visions'". In his recent book, *Leadership: Six Studies in World Strategy*, he accords the highest esteem to leaders with the intellectual courage to be transformative, "who bring virtue at the critical hours of decision and character, which ensures dedication to values over time".

This is a time for those qualities to emerge. ■

THE FIX *Solving Australia's foreign affairs challenges*

Melissa Conley Tyler and Cherie Lagakali on How Australia Can Partner with the Pacific for Digital Resilience and Transformation

"Engaging with the Pacific on digital issues will provide strong security, diplomatic and economic benefits to Australia and the Pacific."

THE PROBLEM: Across the Pacific, technology has changed the way people interact and consume information, disrupting traditional communication practices. Online discussions within and between communities are having real-world effects. Disagreements and misinformation on social media platforms have resulted in cases of violence between villages, vaccine hesitancy and bullying, and TikTok meet-ups have been linked to cases of child abduction and rape. New technology is undermining the already unstable nature of statehood and presenting threats to nations struggling to achieve inclusive and accountable governance.

At the same time, digital technology provides an immense opportunity for the Pacific. There is a deep desire for communities and governments to be better connected globally, which would bring significant change for a region where logistics and connectivity have always been an issue. The COVID-19 pandemic has shown the economic potential of digital connectivity, providing opportunities to interact with global customers while borders were closed and tourism shut down.

Digital technology also enables Pacific nations to maintain notions of statehood, providing opportunities to capture and preserve identity, traditional knowledge, ways of life and culture. For example, Tuvalu, severely impacted by climate change, is rapidly adopting tools and platforms to digitise its culture, heritage and other treasures.

But there is a capability gap due to a lack of digitally skilled people and limitations in the government's capacity to deal with digital technology, which is emerging faster than some governments can understand or regulate. This has created a heavy reliance on outside assistance, increasing opportunities for foreign actors to take advantage of governments.

THE PROPOSAL: Australia must remain a key partner for the Pacific on digital resilience and digital transformation – the ability to withstand incidents and attacks, and the ability to reap the benefits of technological change.

There are several steps that Australia can take to achieve these goals.

First, Australia's government, private sector and civil society should ensure that addressing the digital capability gap is an integral part of their Pacific engagement. In particular, the development community is not seen as an early adopter of digital technology, despite its huge potential to support development outcomes. Some NGOs are embracing the opportunities technology provides, such as partnering with governments on digital cash transfers and with technology companies on improving online literacy and safety. There should be further exploration of such opportunities and how these can be customised to the local context of individual Pacific island countries and integrated within aid programs addressing education, health, climate resilience and economic development.

Second, the Australian government should invest in coordinating cyber activities across its different departments and agencies. The Department of Foreign Affairs and Trade should be better resourced to lead a whole-of-government digital effort in the Pacific, including with the Department of Industry, Science and Resources; the Australian Cyber Security Centre; and the Digital Transformation Agency.

Third, Australia can assist Pacific island countries with coordinating their international assistance programs. Pacific island countries maintain a diverse set of cyber and digital partnerships. But multiple donors have overlapping programs, increasing the burden on Pacific island countries that have limited capacity to engage, coordinate and manage programs. A cultural challenge in saying no to resources has also led to duplication of programs and reduced effectiveness, while incompatible cyber and tech capabilities between countries hamper communication on regional security efforts – for example, in cooperating to combat illegal fishing. Australia can reinforce collaboration with other actors that share similar interests – including the United States, Japan, New Zealand and France.

Fourth, the Australian government should use its diplomatic channels and convening power to facilitate conversations between Pacific governments and the tech industry – such as Meta (Facebook), TikTok and Google – to find ways to address concerns, such as moderation of social media, combating the spread of online misinformation and providing access to platforms for Pacific online journalists. Addressing the Pacific's digital needs and cyber security challenges requires a multistakeholder partnership and common understanding of culturally and socially desirable services, platforms, and terms and conditions.

Finally, as Australia takes steps to boost digital capabilities in the Pacific, it must demonstrate that strengthened engagement in the online space is not purely for its own purposes, but a genuine attempt to build a safer and more secure Pacific. The Australian government should continue to engage with regional forums to build cooperation and to encourage Pacific-led dialogue – including the Pacific Islands Forum Dialogue Partner mechanism and the new Partners in the Blue Pacific initiative.

WHY IT WILL WORK: Engaging with the Pacific on digital issues will provide strong security, diplomatic and economic benefits to Australia and the Pacific.

Physical and digital linkages across the Pacific directly impact Australia's security. This has led to Canberra's strategic investments in the Coral Sea Cable network, underwriting Telstra's acquisition of Pacific telecommunications provider Digicel and a recent memorandum of understanding with Papua New Guinea on cyber security cooperation. Cyber security and digital infrastructure is perceived as a domain of geopolitical competition. But the importance of digital connectivity goes beyond defence and security. A digitally connected Pacific will pay diplomatic dividends for Australia, building better, stronger relationships with the region.

It also makes economic sense. For example, financing undersea cables can lead to decreased internet prices, improved digital services, better connectivity, and a safe and secure online environment for users.

Communities also want it. Pacific regional organisations, governments, businesses and local communities involved in technical capabilities, internet access and online safety all want to engage, not just with "Australia" but with committed Australian individuals and organisations. That spirit needs to be leveraged and cherished.

Most of all, Australia should be involved because digital transformation and resilience is already happening and Australia risks being "the odd one out". For example, the global community of organisations involved in capacity building, the Global Forum on Cyber Expertise, based in The Hague, recently launched a Pacific Hub. A dedicated team of three digital experts from Pacific island countries will become an independent and important source of knowledge, information and advice for Pacific governments, implementers and donor governments on cyber security and safety issues as well as appropriate means of delivering technical assistance.

The volcanic eruption that severed Tonga's undersea cable connection to the outside world earlier this year demonstrated how vulnerable Pacific island countries are in terms of connectivity. But the quick restoration of Tonga's internet access through the commitment of the Tongan community and key stakeholders, including deployment of Starlink low-orbit satellites, shows the potential for coordination and the pace with which the digital environment in the Pacific is evolving. The speed of technological advancement has created a critical time frame for Pacific island countries to become digitally equipped to protect their interests.

If Australia's worst fears regarding the Pacific are about instability, then it should care about the disruptive impact of digital technology. But Australia's greatest hopes should be around the transformational potential of cultural and economic connectivity for Pacific island communities. Its vision should be of a Pacific region that is digitally connected in a secure and safe way that protects governments, societies and communities while allowing access to global cultural conversations, markets and information flows. A safe and prosperous digital environment supports a flourishing Pacific.

THE RESPONSE: The Minister for International Development and the Pacific, Pat Conroy, said he agreed that digital capability was critical for Pacific island countries and that more needed to be done to address cyber risks.

He said Australia had existing programs that were helping to build cyber resilience in the Pacific, including the Cyber and Critical Tech Cooperation Program. Australia also funds the Girls Online (GO!) program to support girls in Vanuatu and Tonga to address cyberbullying and engage safely online.

"We will be examining issues of Pacific digital capability in more detail and will consider enhancing our efforts in this important and emerging field," he said. ■

Reviews

CHINA

Happy Together: Bridging the Australia–China Divide
David Walker and Li Yao with Karen Walker
Melbourne University Publishing

Happy Together is a memoir by David Walker, an Australian historian, and Li Yao, his Chinese friend and translator. As both an Australian story and the story of Australia are set in Chinese contexts, the work also chimes with the finest literary evocations of Chinese history in English. Jonathan Spence's 1978 history of peasant suffering in the seventeenth century, *The Death of Woman Wang*, is one work that, whatever the differences, returns to mind.

Happy Together opens in 1968 with a displaced figure eking out his survival on the back roads that connect Inner Mongolia and Shanxi Province. As familiar there as "drought, poverty and pestilence", this ragged character was the itinerant musician and storyteller Li Zhang, living on charity in the villages and the melancholy strains of his single-string *erhu*:

> Swan goose
> In the sky
> Flying away from us …

Originally a schoolteacher, Li Zhang had been declared a "rightist", someone thought to be against the revolution. Fed up with the indignities he suffered during the Cultural Revolution, he finally left his village in search of the Li family's ancestral home in Shanxi and was never seen again.

Yet his disappearance opens the story's great embrace of human possibilities in the interweaving of Li Yao's story with David's across the Australia–China divide.

Li Zhang was an older cousin of Li Yao. Li Yao was born in 1946 in Li village in Inner Mongolia. The family, which was Han Chinese, had been displaced from Shanxi in the late 1890s when great hunger stalked the land.

Li Yao's great-grandfather Li Dabao decided it was time to go, and they joined the endless procession of the wretched of the Earth. "On the road there were always people ahead, around the next bend, over the next hill and more, always more following … Across his shoulders Li Dabao carried a sturdy pole, a basket hanging at each end. One basket held the littlest children, the other their big iron cooking pot." A bridging sentence follows: "For colonial Australians … such images became the accepted stereotype of the dogged 'Chinaman'."

Conversely, in 1913, we find Australian writer Mary Gaunt travelling in Shanxi. As if retracing the path of the Li family's exodus from the province, and foreshadowing Li Zhang's attempt to return there, she said the roads got "worse and worse". Parallel China–Australia narratives are bitten by the same serpent of human misery that menaces all the world's poor.

The outcome is not always oblivion. The Li family's distress was relieved by land concessions from the Qing government in the grasslands of Inner Mongolia. With careful management by Li Yao's skinflint grandfather, the family did relatively well. Their early settlement grew into Li village. Li Yao's parents, Li Tiren and Li Yueheng, to whom the book is dedicated, were educated in the 1930s, and forward-looking.

One of the "paths" out of "the squalid inequality of early British industrial life" was, as it had been in the Li family's flight from poverty in Shanxi, economic migration. In the 1870s, David's great-great-grandfather William Walker and his wife, Isabella, left Lincolnshire on their exodus to Australia. Bringing their nonconformist strand of Christianity across the world, the Walkers were free settlers in the non-convict colony of South Australia, the "paradise of dissent".

They set up shop in Burra on the edge of the desert, where successful commerce in small goods in the copper-mining community meant that the family "avoided destitution". David was born in 1945 in Adelaide, the son of Gilbert, a schoolteacher, and Glasson, from whom he inherited his gift for language. Like the Li family in

Mongolia, who often thought of their ancestral village in Shanxi, David and family thought from Adelaide back to ancestral Burra.

In *Happy Together*, elemental things, which weave the very disparate Australian and Chinese national, family and personal stories into the same memoir, are consciously evoked: the vast dome of the blue sky above landlocked plains bordering great deserts, such as those of Central Australia and Gobi. Another area in which Australia's past can compete with the depth and breadth of China's is in 60,000 years of Indigenous Australian history that comes with the "Dreaming".

How in that wonderful context did David and Li Yao meet? They met when, after a sustained period of happiness in Australia–China relations, David was appointed to the BHP Chair of Australian Studies at Peking University (from 2013 to 2016).

Once both friends had entered "the world of words", the memoir confides, neither "wanted to leave it". David had studied at Adelaide University and the ANU, become a professor of Australian history, and author of two important books, *Anxious Nation* (1999) and *Stranded Nation* (2017), on a subject that is rather studiously overlooked by his profession: Asian influences in Australian history.

Why, among Australian historians, has David somewhat atypically studied those influences?

Before he became legally blind in 2004, David was unusually short-sighted. Therefore, my suggestion has long been that he was prone to perceive his subject more closely than he otherwise would have. In his mind, I think, the Australianness of Burra, with its scraggy gum trees on the edge of the desert, tended to usurp the town's British cultural heritage. His first memoir, *Not Dark Yet* (2011), tells a story that indicates why his close perception of place doubled as he grew up with a brooding family silence, one that drew his attention to the connection between Asia and Australia. In February 1942 on the island of Ambon, David's uncle Laurie, a Leading Aircraftman in 13 Squadron RAAF, was beheaded by the Japanese.

Happy Together retells that story around a moment in 2013 when, again, David felt the world move beneath him. On a trip to Shenyang, he suddenly realised that he was in what was once Mukden, standing exactly where, on 18

September 1931, the Japanese had blown up one of their own trains, blamed the incident on the Chinese and used it to justify their brutal invasion of northern China. In Inner Mongolia, grievous Li family losses and disruptions followed. Later, standing on the Marco Polo Bridge, outside Beijing, David links the start of the Second Sino-Japanese War on 7 July 1937 to the Walker family's irreparable loss in the vast catastrophe of World War II. "If Australia is ever to become an Asian country," David argues, "it may have to change its date for the outbreak of the Second World War."

Suffering in Li Yao's biography also locates him a little outside the expected square. He displayed early literary leanings and wanted to be a teacher. After the revolution, the "rightist" taint that hung around his parents saw his horizons limited to teacher training at Inner Mongolia Normal University. He studied literature and translation, initially from Russian to Chinese. Later, he witnessed grief that was greater than his own protracted and painful experience of betrayal by provocateurs during "red" cultural rectification. He also felt the monstrous injustices done to his parents.

After political relaxation, he became a journalist. He also managed to remain dedicated to his literary calling. In 1980 he met Perth English teacher Alison Hewitt, and he began to translate Henry Lawson's short story "The Drover's Wife". David and Li Yao became close friends when *Not Dark Yet* became Li Yao's twenty-sixth translation of an Australian book into Chinese, whereupon Li Yao wanted to see his own life in a memoir. In 2016, he revisited the back roads along which his errant cousin Li Zhang had once travelled. This time, however, Li Yao did not disappear; he picked up where Li Zhang left his ghost. Li Yao was also travelling with David and his wife, Karen, as they researched his family history.

Hence, the story that opens out before us.

With some debt to the "Dreaming", one imagines, you'd have to be something of a seer to do what David does: lift an Australian story and history out of the usual British frame and place it in a finely wrought regional – in this case, Chinese cultural – context. And that is an implication of other pieces I've written on the influence of David's legal blindness on his work.

To produce *Happy Together,* David had Karen, whose vital contribution to the book included keeping a photo record and diary details of whom they met and what they saw and where. Unlike Jonathan Spence, David knew no Chinese. But David had Li Yao to supply him with the intimate understandings of his own life and of Chinese history that permitted David, on listening carefully, to narrate this visionary joint memoir in elegant English.

Greg Lockhart

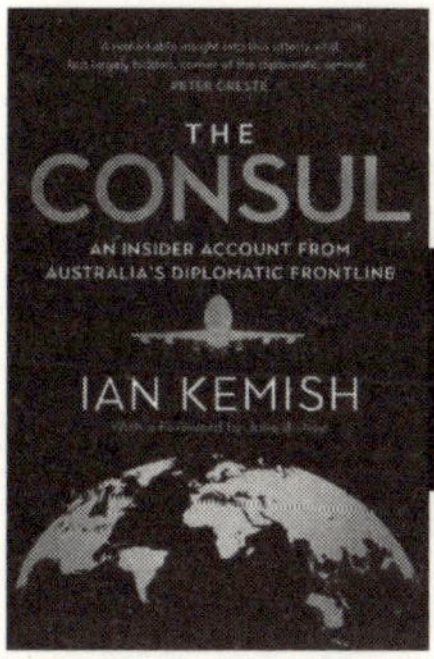

DIPLOMACY

The Consul: An Insider Account from Australia's Diplomatic Frontline
Ian Kemish
University of Queensland Press

On Christmas Eve in 2012, I was leaving New Delhi after three months as an unpaid intern at the UN. Unfortunately, my flight was delayed and I missed my connection in Kuala Lumpur. I stood holding my redundant boarding card, in tears and exhausted after my first experience living in a developing country. I was feeling very depressed about the recent Nirbhaya case – the gang rape and murder of a twenty-three-year-old student on a bus – which had happened close to where I was living. A woman came over to me and asked if I was okay. I wasn't. She gave me her business card and said, "I work for the Australian government – if you need anything at all, please call me." It was all the assurance I needed to get through the next twenty-four hours, before landing at home in time for Christmas Day. The diplomat's name was Caitlin – I am forever grateful to her, and have returned to India many times since.

It's this kind of humanity, albeit through the lens of tragedy, that Ian Kemish conveys in *The Consul*. I found myself poring over every word. From the first few pages, Kemish, a former ambassador and senior diplomat who served as assistant secretary of DFAT's Consular Branch, cleverly establishes that this is not going to be a book of DFAT talking points. He admits straight up that he broke all the rules and ends the first chapter with a heart-wrenching story – building rapport with his reader.

The Consul intertwines personal anecdotes with significant moments in Australia's history that have shaped our national identity. Kemish's narratives include characters with whom many of us are probably familiar, which is partly the power of the book – it's relatable not only for Kemish and his colleagues, but also for the reader. Towards the end of the book, he recalls former Australian foreign minister Stephen Smith's response to the 2008 terror attacks in Mumbai. As I read the words, I found myself transported back to the Taj Mahal Palace Hotel when I visited on a work trip with Smith in 2019. We had walked through the hotel and to the memorial, and he had described what those moments are like when you get that kind of phone call as foreign minister.

There are clear turning points in Kemish's career that were important for him personally, for DFAT and for Australia. Two, in particular, stand out: the September 11 attacks in 2001 and the Bali bombings in 2002. He discusses what they did right, what they did wrong, and how over time these events shaped the Australian government's consular responses to crises. But he does it with such humility and compassion. In his chapter about September 11, Kemish lists by name, age and occupation the ten Australians who were killed. He recalls, with vivid detail, where he was as the first plane hit. Like many of us, I also remember exactly where I was. I was sixteen years old and working at Reading Cinemas in Mandurah, Western Australia. We were about to watch a premiere of *Artificial Intelligence*, in which New York City is flooded. For today's graduates of international relations, such powerful historical narratives might provoke them to consider how they, as the "post-9/11 generation", view the world differently to those who lived through it.

Kemish warns about the geopolitics of the Indo-Pacific and what it means for everyday Australians travelling in the region.

Recalling a helicopter rescue (of which there were many) in the Himalayas in 2003, Kemish explains how a deal was struck with the Nepalese government which involved securing permits from the Chinese government to access the Tibetan side of the world's sixth-highest mountain, Cho Oyu. Securing the permits involved a phone call between the Chinese and (acting) Australian foreign ministers of the day – something that required a relatively functional diplomatic relationship, which Australia and China have not had now for years. The meeting between foreign ministers Penny Wong and Wang Yi on the sidelines of the G20 in July 2022 was the first meeting between Australian and Chinese foreign ministers since 2019 – would the rescue of 2003 have been possible in the last two years? Probably not. Diplomacy might sometimes seem abstract, yet strong diplomatic relationships matter for everyone.

The Consul raises important questions about the role of DFAT and the Australian government, and makes it clear that there is more demand than ever on DFAT and other agencies as more people travel overseas. We are all likely familiar with the debates about the chronic underfunding of DFAT and the need for more resourcing – on reading *The Consul*, one doesn't need much more convincing that this is certainly the case. But perhaps more interestingly, Kemish discusses the different roles of various branches within DFAT. *The Consul* presents a case for Australia's core business abroad being just that – the consulate. I found myself thinking about the priorities of our foreign missions, and how little scope or time there is – whether right or wrong – to deal with education, arts or other forms of soft diplomacy. This was because of the sheer resource constraint (both financial and human) and the significant emotional labour required to deliver on Australians' (too high) expectations.

While this book may sound like one for the policy wonks of Australia, its audience should extend to leadership circles in any industry. There is a lot to be learnt from Kemish's brutal honesty about his failings as a leader, but also his successes. We learn about the times Kemish had to make decisions between two bad choices, how hierarchy manifests (or doesn't) in a crisis, and how it can take a crisis for leadership to emerge. That seems to be the case for Kemish – he became a leader when outgoing ambassador to Indonesia Ric Smith rang him at 3 a.m. at the time of the Bali bombings.

Many of the major events in *The Consul* we know from the media or our own understanding of Australia's history. But Kemish gives us a behind-the-scenes look at Australia's response to these. He also highlights the sheer depth and breadth of work DFAT does that we never hear about. I finished the book wondering how Kemish feels today. I wondered about our national history and thus our collective trauma that people like Kemish and his colleagues carry with them. We might joke about public servants leaving the office at 5.01 p.m., but figures such as Kemish have never clocked off.

Erin Watson

Correspondence

"Testing Ground" by Allan Gyngell

Huong Le Thu

Allan Gyngell's article gives an eloquent overview of the evolution of South-East Asia's position in Australia's strategic thinking. Gyngell reminds us of the importance of South-East Asia for Australia and highlights the trajectory of the not-always-easy, but still relatively successful, story of our relations. It's hard to disagree with the premise that the new Labor government ought to "do more" in the region. But his article stops at spelling out what new approaches Australia should take. We should not expect more of the same, just with greater intensity. More of the same is not going to suffice in the current environment.

With the new government in place, there is an opportunity for a reset. The Albanese government made a strong start with visits to the region and saying the right things, setting a better tone. Both Prime Minister Albanese and Foreign Minister Wong promised closer attention to South-East Asia and the Pacific, and thus far their style of engagement seems more respectful and open to listening. But how the reset will be achieved is yet to be shaped.

There are three ways that Australia could rebuild and reset its foreign policy in the region:

1. Revive its traditional position and image as a benign, engaging middle power, strong on development aid, education and multilateral diplomacy – an approach in projecting Australia abroad that was practised, particularly by Labor, for decades.
2. Continue the new path set by the former Coalition government of a more muscular, hard-security-focused balancer – an active, even hawkish, strategic actor.
3. Invent a new approach that is a mixture of both.

The first approach is difficult and would require serious reshuffling of resources, including increased budget allocation to DFAT, and stronger popular support. It is relatively easy to drift towards the second pathway, given Australia's current posturing, the defence procurement commitments continued under the Labor government (like nuclear-powered submarines under the AUKUS agreement), the public support for a more robust approach vis-a-vis China, and a general sense of a growing threat to the international security and economic environment. The third one, which seems the most logical to me, may require the most thinking and planning in order to get the mixture right – the balance and proportion – and to reach a bipartisan consensus for a new long-term strategy.

Australia's strengths in South-East Asia have been its contribution to development, gender equality, education and capacity building, agri-tech, and emerging areas of renewable energy assistance. The new muscular Australia has been criticised in some capitals while appreciated in others. But it will be difficult for this to be Australia's strongest suit – Canberra has not been seen as a key security actor in the region. Not alone. If anything, Australia may be viewed as influential when acting with others. But its military capacity, size and pre-existing security arrangements with great powers will prevent this side of its strategic personality becoming its main strength. It has the advantage of close and trusted reactions with significant actors, like the US and Japan. But it is not always seen as completely independent.

In the policy debate, those, like Gyngell, who are conscious of regional opinions are often too critical of Canberra's conduct, amplifying the criticism from some South-East Asian neighbours – including Indonesia's critical reaction to the AUKUS announcements – which they tend to view as reflecting an overall regional negativity. Too often Australia downplays the positive stories and its positive image abroad. For Vietnam, as an example, there's hardly anything negative that can be said about Australia, whether within the context of strategic conversations or citizens' day-to-day perceptions. Self-criticism, or self-correcting, should not overcorrect based on one view or criticism only, because it can lead to Australia undoing what it's been doing well. It is important for Australia to be able to recognise its strengths, benefit from these and adjust according to the current need and how Australia wants to steer its future role and image in the region.

Australia should have a guiding framework for engagement, based on the shared goals of the region – stability and prosperity. But it is crucial to understand the group dynamics in South-East Asia and be sensitive to any prioritisation that may be perceived as divisive or dismissive of ASEAN's centrality. Australia, like any country, including the ASEAN member states themselves, should tailor its strategy to the partner with whom it is engaging. The worldviews, security outlook and strategies of individual actors are clearly diverging. Different agendas need different partners. Individual sensitivities, needs and priorities vary, and Canberra should be able to respond to, and engage with, each accordingly. The hierarchy of Australia's bilateral relationships in South-East Asia that Gyngell details should be revised, so that it is not based purely on the historical predisposition of individual partners, but on their current agendas, and correspondent to their receptiveness to and appetite for closer ties.

I share Gyngell's conviction that Australia – as South-East Asia's immediate neighbour – cannot afford an optional or fluctuating engagement with the region. The reset is not just about this government, but involves a big and long-term question: what image and role does Australia want to project and live up to, now and for years to come? Building a national brand takes time and commitment, but needs to be pursued with urgency. There is a greater expectation from this government than from the previous one – especially with Penny Wong as the first foreign minister of South-East Asian heritage – to lead the new chapter of Australia's foreign policy.

Huong Le Thu is the principal fellow at Perth USAsia Centre. She is a non-resident fellow at the Centre for Strategic and International Studies, Washington DC, Southeast Asia Program, and a member of the Advisory Board of the Griffith Asia Institute, Griffith University.

Marc Purcell and Michael Wesley

In his essay "Testing Ground", Allan Gyngell rightly calls on Australia to engage with South-East Asian leaders on what matters to them. And what matters is growth. Development connects Australia with one of the region's most important priorities. Development assistance must be a key part of Australia's statecraft in South-East Asia.

In a competitive region, development assistance provides the basis for dialogue and cooperation with neighbours on tackling their development challenges – using Australian knowledge and goodwill to strengthen relations. Decades of gyrations in development spending are a sign of Australia's foreign policy immaturity. We need a bipartisan commitment to our aid approach.

At times, Australia's prime ministers have harnessed development assistance to national interest priorities to good effect. Following the Timor-Leste referendum, John Howard repaired fractured relations with the Jakarta elite with a A$1 billion humanitarian package of grant and loans in response to the Aceh tsunami catastrophe in 2004–05.

In 2007, from Opposition, Kevin Rudd pledged to lift Australia's development spend to 0.5 per cent of gross national income by 2015. Victorious, he harnessed a UN Security Council bid to foreign policy goals, and the Australian aid program was turbocharged and went wider than ever before, reaching even to the Caribbean and West Africa.

But then this leadership on development stalled. In 2013, Julie Bishop controversially abolished AusAID and integrated it into the Department of Foreign Affairs and Trade (DFAT), with consequent loss of aid expertise and capacity to engage in global development discussions. In 2014, she presided helplessly over the largest cuts to DFAT and development assistance in history, when the A$5 billion program was raided, resulting in a A$1 billion reduction. The ensuing cuts included 30 per cent culled from South-East Asia programs, affecting relationships in health and education across Asia. Australia, surrounded by developing countries, declined from thirteenth to twenty-first in OECD aid donors.

Years of hunger games followed, with development a poor cousin to cashed-up defence, despite questions around whether the big talk and spend on defence has much to show for it. We have also under-resourced diplomacy, with a diminished diplomatic footprint. Given the scale of the challenges, development, diplomacy and defence each needs its own internal review, and then we need to think about how to knit them all together.

Ironically, it was the depth of the cuts that saw the rebirth of a national interest case for development assistance to South-East Asia. In the wake of the axing of bilateral health programs, the heightened risk to Australia from diseases and zoonoses allowed the launch of the Indo-Pacific Centre for Health Security in 2017.

Then, in 2020, galvanised by the COVID-19 pandemic and rising anxiety about Chinese influence in our region, development assistance was restored. It became apparent that the ASEAN economies had been belly-whacked economically and socially by the pandemic, and that our economic recovery was tied to theirs. In the words of Woolworths chair Gordon Cairns, "Australia cannot recover well if our neighbouring region is destabilised and deteriorating."

In a series of announcements, the Morrison government increased development assistance by over a billion dollars through temporary targeted measures for the economic and social impacts of COVID-19 in South-East Asia and the Pacific. Over A$300 million was directed to working with Mekong countries, including on the downstream impacts of Chinese dam building. Winning hearts and minds in South-East Asia with development assistance was back in fashion.

At the 2022 election, aid was an issue for the first time since 2007, as the ALP announced A$470 million over four years for South-East Asia. In his first week as prime minister, Anthony Albanese stated, "The truth is that international aid is not only the right thing to do for developing countries, it is in our national interest to engage and to provide support to developing nations." Minister for Foreign Affairs Penny Wong has pledged to rebuild DFAT's diplomatic and development capabilities, saying: "I believe a generous, effective and targeted aid program is fundamental to our engagement with the world." Minister for International Development and the Pacific Pat Conroy has committed that the development spend will increase every year, including through the budget this year.

In a region with economies damaged by the pandemic and a heightened risk of social instability, Australia's development assistance in South-East Asia helps tackle basic livelihood challenges and improve the health and education of the current and coming generations.

As public private models of energy transition and climate adaptation take off, development assistance enables Australia to co-invest and be a partner in tackling common challenges. The new government is pursuing a Development Finance Review, exploring forms of non-grant aid, such as loans and co-investment, that could allow Australia to participate in different forms of commercial development ventures in Asia.

In a competitive space for regional relationships and influence, we can use development assistance to support Australia's national interests in South-East Asia, or watch our national interest go down with our development spend. A new statecraft for Australia in South-East Asia is incomplete without development at its heart.

Marc Purcell and Michael Wesley are co-chairs of the Asia-Pacific Development, Diplomacy & Defence Dialogue (AP4D). Marc is CEO of the Australian Council for International Development (ACFID) and Michael is Deputy Vice-Chancellor International at the University of Melbourne.

Allan Gyngell responds

I am grateful to Huong Le Thu, Marc Purcell and Michael Wesley for their thoughtful responses to my essay.

Le Thu shares my views on South-East Asia's importance to Australia but thinks I should have been more specific about what I want Australia to do in the region. That's a fair point, and I agree with her that "more of the same, just with greater intensity" is not going to be an effective policy in the current environment. In my defence, my basic purpose in the essay was to clear away some of the misconceptions that inhibit our capacity to influence outcomes in the region.

Le Thu suggests Australian policy should mix together what she sees as two different elements from earlier Australian approaches. The first, which she associates mostly with Labor governments, is to revive Australia's reputation as the "benign, engaging middle power, strong on development aid, education and multilateral democracy". The other strand is the more "muscular, hard-security-focused" approach of the previous Coalition. I take this to mean Australian support in South-East Asia for shoring up the more forthright American and Japanese responses to China.

I don't see the benign versus muscular division quite as sharply as she does. Elements of both approaches have been present in the policies of most Australian governments over the years. And responses to China's presence and ambitions have featured all the way back to the Malayan Emergency in the 1950s and through the Cambodian peace settlement.

It would be good to hear more from Le Thu about how a different mix would work. For example, she suggests that "the hierarchy of Australia's bilateral relationships in South-East Asia ... should be revised", but without nominating particular changes.

For reasons of geography, economic weight and population size, Indonesia will always top any hierarchy of Australian bilateral relationships in South-East Asia. For the rest of it, however, I see Australia's current relations with other ASEAN states very much mirroring her call to develop relationships based on "their current agendas and correspondent to their receptiveness to and appetite for closer ties". In fact, that dynamic probably sustains all foreign relations.

Le Thu thinks I am too critical of Canberra's past conduct in the region and that in doing so I amplify the criticisms of some Asian neighbours and underplay sympathy in the region for Australia's position. Although I did not try in my essay to categorise South-East Asian views of Australia, which vary widely, I agree with her that our relationship with significant partners like the United States and Japan does give Australia additional weight and respect in its dealings with other South-East Asian countries.

My criticism of the last Coalition government was of its lack of sustained attention to South-East Asia, and the extent to which it saw the region – or so it seemed to me – largely through the prism of global geopolitics and US–China relations. There is much more on offer to Australia here.

Le Thu ends with an important question: "What image and role does Australia want to project and live up to, now and for years to come?" The new foreign minister, Penny Wong, has already tried in speeches around the region to answer it. My own response is that the image should be one of who we are – a successful, stable, multicultural democracy which understands the individual and collective interests of our South-East Asian neighbours. Our role, at least in part, should be to work with those neighbours to construct a peaceful, prosperous region in which all voices are heard, and where rules, which all have contributed to setting, are followed.

Marc Purcell and Michael Wesley begin their argument for more serious attention to aid in Australia's relationships with South-East Asia with an important point: growth is central to all the ASEAN countries. I agree that the slashing of Australian development assistance budgets after 2014, including a 30 per cent cut in South-East Asian programs, damaged Australia's reputation as a reliable regional partner.

A problem for supporters of the aid program is that they must contend with two different narratives shaping the public view of South-East Asia. One story emphasises the 36 million South-East Asians still living in absolute poverty, mostly in villages in Indonesia and the Philippines, and their ongoing health and education needs. The other focuses on the burgeoning economic growth of the region's great cities and the 350 million people in its expanding middle class. "Why is Australian aid needed here?" visiting policymakers sometimes ask.

This diversity means that the Australian aid program in South-East Asia needs to address a wide range of development goals, from humanitarian relief and poverty reduction to general economic cooperation. Traditional aid merges with new approaches which, Purcell and Wesley note, "could enable Australia to participate in different forms of non-grant aid, such as loans and co-investment".

And, of course, growth will never come principally through the aid program, but through conventional patterns of investment and trade. These are areas where Australia still lags badly.

The integrated Australian approach to its international relationships which Purcell and Wesley have pursued in their joint chairing of the innovative Asia-Pacific Development, Diplomacy & Defence Dialogue (AP4D) has been an encouraging step for everyone interested in drawing on all the elements of Australian national power to build purposeful relations with the states of South-East Asia.

Allan Gyngell is national president of the Australian Institute of International Affairs.

Correspondence

"The Ukraine War" by Sheila Fitzpatrick

Matthew Sussex

As a sometimes-frustrated Russia hand, I found it refreshing to see AFA publish a contribution on the war in Ukraine ("The Ukraine war: Does anyone want it to end?", Issue 15) from Sheila Fitzpatrick, Australia's foremost historian of the USSR. Her extensive achievements and standing in the academic community give her words influence: even more so in a country where the ranks of specialists on Russia regrettably continue to thin.

It is a great pity, then, that Fitzpatrick decided to uncritically repeat some popular but demonstrably incorrect judgements on the origins of the war, married to some coy and equally flawed hints about the intentions of its main players. Upon reading her assessment one could easily conclude that the Anglophone world was at primary fault for the death and destruction caused in Ukraine, rather than the man who actually started it. Having a bet each way, she claims Vladimir Putin's motives are unknowable, and yet were apparently driven by "NATO's encouragement of Ukraine's application for membership".

Fitzpatrick's seeming desire to give Putin a free pass goes beyond the loaded title, in which she assumes (and then later asserts, with no actual evidence, instead resorting to an old throwaway trope about the US military-industrial complex), that the West is seeking to prolong the war for as long as possible to "punish" Putin.

As Fitzpatrick puts it, "Europe and the Anglophone world ('the West') appear united in their desire to punish Russia, but there seems to be no similar resolve about trying to end the war." And yet, perversely, because Putin cannot "just stop, even if he wants to", the implication is that it is up to Ukraine – and the West by extension – to offer him inducements to do so.

Unfortunately, that line of thinking is detached from reality.

To begin with, we know why Putin invaded. He has told us. Comparing himself to Peter the Great, he said in early June that it was now once again "time to take back what is ours". Earlier he wrote that Ukrainians have no separate identity to Russians and only deserve true sovereignty in partnership with Russia. His foreign minister, Sergey Lavrov, has called for regime change, and described the removal of Volodymyr Zelenskyy as a specific war aim in early July. Russia's former president and prime minister Dmitry Medvedev has called Georgia and Kazakhstan "artificial creations". And Russia's state media is replete with neo-colonial rhetoric about Russia's "reunification" with Ukraine. It has eagerly fetishised military conquest via the infamous and improvised 'Z' symbol, has sought to justify mass killings, summary executions and rape, and has called for Ukrainians to be liquidated.

All wars have many causes: deep or structural ones, intermediate ones, and precipitating sparks. But there should be little doubt that this one (following the Russian invasion of 2014 in the midst of a democratic revolution in Ukraine) is a war of Russian imperial expansion rather than a response to NATO enlargement. That's because NATO has effectively frozen Ukraine's NATO aspirations. Germany scuppered the necessarily unanimous support for it, and there has been little enthusiasm to push the issue, either prior to Putin's invasion or at NATO's Madrid summit in June.

It's true, as Fitzpatrick asserts, that Russian objections to NATO's continued existence, let alone its growth, were persistent in post-Soviet Russia. But Moscow did not formally oppose Eastern European nations joining the alliance, and indeed Boris Yeltsin's Russia sought to build stable ties with the alliance through the 1994 Partnership for Peace and the 1997 *NATO-Russia Founding Act*. Putin himself has repeatedly said Russia "did not see a problem" with NATO enlarging, a point Fitzpatrick is silent on. And when Finland and Sweden abandoned their long-held neutrality and announced they were applying for membership, Putin did little more than shrug.

This is instructive, because Putin clearly sees NATO posing a normative challenge to his regime and his political fortunes, rather than any existential security threat. While those may be synonymous in his mind, Putin's lack of interest in diplomacy before invading, the brutal acts carried out by his forces and his shifting war aims show that he cares little how his actions are perceived. Crucially, and contrary to Fitzpatrick's argument, Putin has made it impossible for Zelenskyy to do anything other than fight for Ukraine's national survival.

Fitzpatrick's claim that the US and Europe are seeking to prolong the war is equally dubious, especially given that the conflict has diverted US attention away from the more pressing challenge of strategic competition with China. Indeed, American and European fears about provoking Putin have engendered a strategy of de-escalation at any cost for over a decade. Biden explicitly telegraphed to Putin that NATO would not intervene militarily under any circumstances. And since the invasion, a host of leaders from Macron to Scholz – and Biden – have sought to offer diplomatic off-ramps to a Kremlin manifestly uninterested in them.

In contrast, it has been Putin who has sought out prolonged confrontation, and now conflict. He has done so through the creation of vulnerable European overdependencies, the weaponisation of energy, and nuclear threats. Meanwhile his political warfare campaign has been designed to hasten the fragmentation of a West that he sees as destined for history's ash heap.

Given that record, Fitzpatrick's concluding complaint about the West launching a "mischievous new Putin-baiting campaign" to needle him and make "life uncomfortable for Russians" is bizarre. But it provides an insight into the caricatured analysis that she has produced here. In trying to pin Europe's first land war in over eighty years on a cynical West determined to see it continue, she has unfortunately missed the biggest cynic of the lot. It is not Biden, Zelenskyy or the EU, but Putin who has the sole power – yet evidently no wish – to stop it.

Matthew Sussex is senior fellow at the Centre for Defence Research, and associate professor (adjunct) at the Griffith Asia Institute.

Sheila Fitzpatrick responds

Certainly Vladimir Putin started the war in Ukraine, as is clearly stated in my article. One may therefore say, as Matthew Sussex does, that it is up to Putin to end it. But no serious diplomat or statesperson would accept Sussex's premise that, in the real world, such outcomes are achieved totally unilaterally. Think of the Cuban Missile Crisis for an example of behind-the-scenes back-channel negotiations that got the United States, the Soviet Union and the world out of a very dangerous situation.

We are in a dangerous situation now, especially since the Zaporizhzhia nuclear power plant has come into the line of fire. There is (probably) no harm in taking a public stance of unbending non-negotiability à la Sussex, especially as Australia, not being directly threatened, can afford a degree of irresponsibility. It should be remembered, however, that what is happening in Ukraine is not a war game but an actual war, inflicting huge amounts of suffering and damage on Ukraine and putting the whole of Europe in jeopardy. Stopping the war as soon as possible is of the highest importance, and that can only be done by finding terms on which Ukraine, Europe and Russia (and, realistically, the US) can agree.

My hope – and the central point of my article – is that there are some modern-day, hard-nosed but realistic Henry Kissingers working behind the scenes to find those terms.

Sheila Fitzpatrick's most recent book is The Shortest History of the Soviet Union.

Back Issues

ALL PRICES INCLUDE GST, POSTAGE AND HANDLING.

- ☐ **AFA1** ($19.99) The Big Picture
- ☐ **AFA2** ($19.99) Trump in Asia
- ☐ **AFA3** ($19.99) Australia & Indonesia
- ☐ **AFA4** ($19.99) Defending Australia
- ☐ **AFA5** ($19.99) Are We Asian Yet?
- ☐ **AFA6** ($19.99) Our Sphere of Influence
- ☐ **AFA7** ($19.99) China Dependence
- ☐ **AFA8** ($19.99) Can We Trust America?
- ☐ **AFA9** ($19.99) Spy vs Spy
- ☐ **AFA10** ($19.99) Friends, Allies and Enemies
- ☐ **AFA11** ($19.99) The March of Autocracy
- ☐ **AFA12** ($19.99) Feeling the Heat
- ☐ **AFA13** ($19.99) India Rising?
- ☐ **AFA14** ($22.99) The Taiwan Choice
- ☐ **AFA15** ($22.99) Our Unstable Neighbourhood

PAYMENT DETAILS I enclose a cheque/money order made out to Schwartz Books Pty Ltd.
Or please debit my credit card (MasterCard, Visa or Amex accepted).

CARD NO. ☐☐☐☐☐☐☐☐☐☐☐☐☐☐☐☐

EXPIRY DATE ____ / ____ CCV ____ AMOUNT $ ____

CARDHOLDER'S NAME ____

SIGNATURE ____

NAME ____

ADDRESS ____

EMAIL ____ PHONE ____

Post or fax this form to: Reply Paid 90094, Collingwood VIC 3066 **Freecall:** 1800 077 514 **or** +61 3 9486 0288
Fax: (03) 9011 6106 **Email:** subscribe@australianforeignaffairs.com **Website:** australianforeignaffairs.com
Subscribe online at australianforeignaffairs.com/subscribe (please do not send electronic scans of this form)

The Back Page

FOREIGN POLICY CONCEPTS AND JARGON, EXPLAINED

STRATEGIC EQUILIBRIUM

What is it: An approach to foreign policy sometimes contrasted with balance of power models. Along with related terms like "international equilibrium", it has been used on and off since the 1950s.

Who uses it: Penny Wong (foreign minister, Australia) used the term in her first public speech in the role. She envisioned Asia as a region "where disputes are guided by international law and norms, not by power and size". On top of traditional structures like ASEAN, sovereign nations would be free to pursue other agreements. "Strategic equilibrium enables countries to make their own sovereign choices," she said, "rather than having their future decided for them."

Why now: Strategic equilibrium can come into vogue when institutional agreements decline in strength. It offers a more free-wheeling model of managing rising Chinese power in the Asia-Pacific, advocated for by the likes of Michael J. Green (CEO, US Studies Centre).

Where does it come from: It originates with game theory, a branch of mathematics and related practice that discerns optimal (and suboptimal) behaviour in rational actors. It was applied to foreign policy, with mixed results, partly thanks to Thomas Schelling (economist and Nobel laureate, University of Maryland).

Does it work: Not really. Paul Musgrave (political scientist, University of Massachusetts Amherst) has criticised game theory's application to foreign policy as a tool "to make the Cold War seem easy to manage" that degenerated statecraft "into recondite academic parlor games". Its return is well-timed: a hazy term applied to a place and period increasingly defined by uncertainty.